A Guide to the Norfolk Way

Books by David H. Kennett

Anglo-Saxon pottery
Portrait of Bedfordshire
Victorian and Edwardian horses from historic photographs
Norfolk villages
Barracuda guide to county history. Volume V: Bedfordshire

David H. Kennett

A guide to
The Norfolk Way

Constable London

First published in Great Britain 1983
by Constable & Company Ltd
10 Orange Street London WC2H 7EG
Copyright © 1983 David H. Kennett
ISBN 0 09 463030 5
Set in Times New Roman 9pt
by Inforum Ltd, Portsmouth
Printed in Great Britain by
BAS Printer Ltd, Over Wallop
Hampshire

Contents

Illustrations

On all maps north is at the top of the page

KEY TO MAPS

The Route

Road

Track

Railway line

River and direction of flow

Coast

Building

Church

Windmill

Lighthouse

Urban area

Bacton Gas Terminal

Earthwork

Trees/Woodland

Acknowledgements

The making of a book is a difficult process and my thanks are many. Those courteous people, the men and women of Norfolk, deserve my thanks for their salutations as we passed when walking. An especial group deserves particular thanks, the employees of the Eastern Counties Omnibus Company who set me down at points on the way. Librarians in Luton, Bedford, Norwich and Yarmouth have helped in ways too numerous to mention to track odd facts mentioned in the book. My parents endured my presence for weeks on end while I went out to walk each day and came back late each night: for two years my visits home were for little more than to use their house as a base. My only regret is that my father did not live to see the book he had so helped to make.

I have been fortunate in my publishers and thank Elfreda Powell, Carola Piggott and Miles Huddleston for their assistance. When a delay occurred in the production of the text of this book their patience was considerable.

For the support of my friends at one period I am particularly grateful.

David H. Kennett
St Thomas the Apostle, 1982

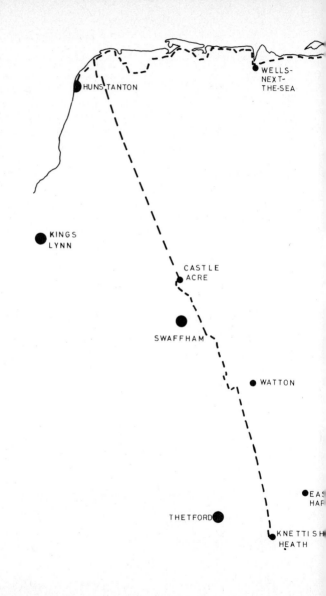

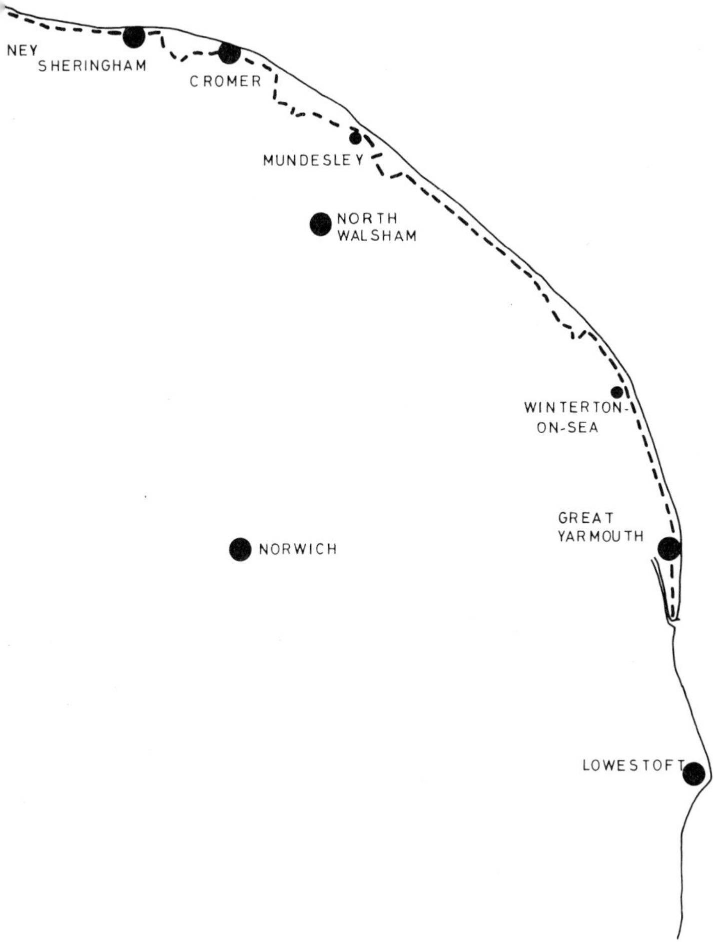

NEY
SHERINGHAM
CROMER
MUNDESLEY
NORTH
WALSHAM
WINTERTON-
ON-SEA
GREAT
YARMOUTH
NORWICH
LOWESTOFT

Introduction

The Norfolk Way is a convenient description of Britain's newest long-distance footpath. The official title is Peddars Way and the Norfolk Coast Path. Both portions of the Way, as well as the route described from Cromer to Great Yarmouth, had been accessible to walkers for a long time before the route was considered by the Countryside Commission in 1979–81. It was approved as Britain's tenth long-distance walk in March 1982.

The first part of the Norfolk Way is Peddars Way from Knettishall Heath, east of Thetford, to Holme-next-the-Sea, north-east of Hunstanton. It follows the line of a Roman road which originally ran from Colchester to Lincoln. South of Peddars Way, in Suffolk, the route can be traced in parish boundaries. In Norfolk, Peddars Way is used as the parish boundary of no fewer than thirty parishes from West Harling to Old Hunstanton. Significantly, it is only where the original route has been completely lost between Threxton and North Pickenham that Peddars Way is not used as a parish boundary. This section has been replaced by a walk agreed between the Countryside Commission, the Norfolk County Council and local landowners so that it is possible to walk from south to north uninterrupted.

The second part of the Norfolk Way is the Norfolk Coast Path from Hunstanton to Cromer which follows the coastline of north Norfolk. Only between Thornham and Brancaster and between Sheringham and Cromer are detours made inland.

The third part of the Norfolk Way is not yet designated as part of the long-distance walk but follows public footpaths, mainly along the coast, from Cromer to Great Yarmouth.

There are a number of ways in which the Norfolk Way can be walked. One is to do it against the clock, so to speak. Since it is relatively short – the official route of Peddars Way and the Norfolk Coast Path is only 151.2 km (94½ miles), and the Cromer to Yarmouth walk is 63.0 km (39¼ miles) – an experienced walker could complete the whole route in as little as seven days, but there would not be much enjoyment in this.

It can be done in a more leisurely fashion in ten days to a fortnight, which gives time to visit places of interest, wander off the route a bit and relax, taking in the scenery and the views. Many of the sections suggested in this book are pleasant day walks in their own right. On Peddars Way, I would particularly recommend Bridgham to Threxton and North Pickenham to Castle Acre, while on the coast Wells to Blakeney (or Cley-next-the-Sea) and Cley to Sheringham (or on to Cromer) are particularly good sections, as they have good public transport at both ends.

The great delight of the Norfolk Way is that it takes the walker over so much of that very varied county. It begins in Breckland and then crosses the great emptiness of north Norfolk. Between Hunstanton and Weybourne the coast is fairly low-lying, with extensive marshes on the seaward side between Cley-next-the-Sea and within the sea bank thereafter. After Weybourne, the coast is hilly as far as the lost village of Eccles between Happisburgh and Sea Palling. Thereafter it is low-lying. For an outsider who knows little of the county, walking the Norfolk Way provides an excellent introduction to the tranquillity of Norfolk. The resident of the county will find new insights by doing the walk.

There is no best time to walk the Norfolk Way. I have walked parts of it, both in Breckland and along the coast, on bright but cold days in March and November. I have even enjoyed a pleasant day's walk across a different area of the Norfolk countryside in mid-December: it wasn't raining and the sun was visible. My personal preferences are for March to May, and September and October. Nevertheless, I have walked much of the route in July and August, and this has the advantage that the coast buses are in operation in these months, so that access is made easier.

Walking the Norfolk Way, especially Peddars Way, does have one drawback in high summer. It is very hot in Breckland in June, July and August since there is very little rainfall, and in this part of East Anglia which is furthest from the coast there is little of the cooling breeze found on Peddars Way north of Castle Acre and on the Norfolk Coast Path.

A different weather hazard is found on the coast, especially between Weybourne and Happisburgh. This is sea fog, which may take until mid-afternoon to lift. It can be fairly dense and limit visibility to under 30 metres. I have also experienced sandstorms on this section of the coast and inland from it at Trunch. The part of the coast between Cromer and Mundesley is windier than that west of Cromer or that south-east of Mundesley.

Plan of the book

The Norfok Way falls naturally into two sections, with a third which is not yet a designated long-distance walk. Each forms a section of this book. They are preceded by a section giving details of how to join the Norfolk Way from each of the principal towns with railway stations.

There is no logical reason for walking the Norfolk Way from south to north along Peddars Way and then from west to east along the Norfolk Coast Path and the Cromer to Yarmouth walk. It can just as easily be done the opposite way. If a trial run is being made, Peddars Way from Ringstead south to the A148 is a good introduction which is accessible at either end by public transport to or from King's Lynn. An alternative is from Castle Acre south to the A47 or to the vicinity of Saham Toney. In some ways, the coast walk is preferable going from east to west.

The author chose to walk from south to north for two reasons. The first is that there is a recurring sense of discovery in going in this direction: for instance, in ascending the long incline of Peddars Way north of the Thetford to Norwich railway line, or in the view across the River Nar of Castle Acre Priory, and the view of the sea when first seen south of Ringstead. Along the coast, there is the feeling of achievement on climbing Skelding Hill, west of Sheringham, and looking back all the way along the coast to see where one has walked, with Blakeney church visible in a gap in the trees. On a good day, the coast can be seen all the way back to Wells. The second reason is that approaches to the Norfolk Way by public transport are marginally better when starting in the south.

Safety and Equipment

Care should be exercised at all times. This is especially so on the coastal walks. The cliffs at Sheringham, West Runton, Cromer and Overstrand are liable to slip. Do not walk too near the edge. On Peddars Way, the main danger is from a sprained ankle. The part across the sandy area of Breckland has the occasional rabbit warren.

Footwear

Walking boots are usually recommended by authors of guides to long-distance walks. For the Norfolk Way, they are not strictly necessary. The author walked all the route wearing normal walking shoes. Overshoes or wellington boots may be of advantage on Branchester Marsh as this is often very wet, even in dry months like June, July and August.

Clothing

Clothing is very much a personal matter. Walk in what you feel comfortable wearing. Good socks are essential and a supply should be carried. Never walk two days in the same pair of socks. Ladies are advised to wear slacks, although some people (of both sexes) prefer shorts.

An outer jacket is desirable, partly because of the pockets, but it is personal preference whether a man wears an anorak or an ordinary sports coat. A lightweight mackintosh should be carried, preferably one which when rolled up will occupy only a small space. A long-sleeved pullover is also worth taking along, especially on the coastal sections, as there can be quite piercing winds. A woollen hat is useful, partly to keep the ears warm if the wind turns cold.

Rucksack

A rucksack is a most useful piece of equipment and several different types are available. Those intending to seek bed-and-breakfast type accommodation each night can make do with a fairly small, light one. A duffle bag, particularly if a little larger than normal and with a map pocket, will suffice. Those intending to camp are advised to equip themselves with a tubular-frame rucksack which allows the weight to be carried on the haunches rather than on the shoulders. It also keeps the sack away from the walker's back.

Maps

A good set of the relevant Ordnance Survey maps will add to the walker's enjoyment of the Norfolk Way.

The former 1 inch to 1 mile series covered the route on sheets

124 King's Lynn
125 Fakenham
126 North Walsham
136 Great Yarmouth

Some find these preferable to the more recent 1:50,000 series.

On the 1:50,000 series, the Norfolk Way is covered by maps

132 North-west Norfolk
133 North-east Norfolk
134 Norwich and the Broads
144 Thetford and Breckland

At the time of writing the 1:25,000 Second Series is available for only one portion of the Norfolk Way:

TG 23–33 Cromer

This is a most useful map to acquire for walking the first part of the Cromer to Great Yarmouth walk.

The older 1:25,000 First Series is still available for the remainder of the route. Relevant sheets for Peddars Way are:

TL 98, TL 99, TL 89,
TF 80 (but here the route is essentially along new paths),
TF 81, TF 71 (small portion only), TF 72, TF 73, TF 64/74.

Relevant sheets for the Norfolk Coast Path are:

TF 64/74 Hunstanton
TF 84 Burnham Market
TF 94 Wells-next-the-Sea
TG 04 Blakeney
TG 14 Sheringham (this includes Cromer within TG 24)

Relevant sheets for the Cromer to Yarmouth walk are:

TG 32 Sea Palling
TG 42 Hickling
TG 41 Winterton-on-Sea
TG 51 Caister-on-Sea
TG 50 Great Yarmouth

   These sheets will eventually be replaced by the following sheets
of the 1:25,000 Second Series maps:
   TL 88/98; TL 89/99
   TF 80/90; TF 81/91; TF 61/71; TF 62/72; TF 63/73
   TF 64/74; TF 84/94
   TG 04/14; TG 23/33; TG 22/32; TG 42; TG 41/51; TG 40/50
As the already published sheet TG 23/33 makes clear, these will be
of great value to walkers, and when available their purchase is to be
recommended.

Compass
Although not strictly necessary, it is useful for the walker to have a
compass in his rucksack. This is especially so on the coastal sections
which can be misty in the mornings (thick fog is not unknown at 11
a.m. in April). Make sure you know how to use a modern Silva-type
compass if you carry one.

The National Grid
This is explained on each sheet of the Ordnance Survey Map.

Admission times
The standard Department of the Environment hours for admission
to Ancient Monuments in their care are:

	Weekdays	Sundays
Nov.–Feb.	09.30 – 16.00	14.00 – 16.00
Mar, Apr., Oct.	09.30 – 17.30	14.00 – 17.30
May–Sept.	09.30 – 19.00	14.00 – 19.00

Other admission times are given in the Information notes to each
section.

The Country Code
1 Guard against fire risks
2 Fasten all gates
3 Keep dogs under proper control
4 Keep to paths across farm land
5 Avoid damaging fences, hedges and walls
6 Leave no litter
7 Safeguard water supplies
8 Protect wild life, wild plants and trees
9 Go carefully on country roads
10 Respect the life of the countryside

Part One: Approaches to the Norfolk Way

The isolation of the Norfolk Way from the major towns of Norfolk is one of its charms. However, this does make it necessary to give directions as to how to arrive at a suitable point on the route to begin walking. It is assumed that those who wish to walk the whole route have arrived in the county by train or by long-distance coach. Even so, before beginning to walk the Norfolk Way, the walker may have either a long bus journey or a walk of several kilometres from a station or a bus terminus. Beginning in Norwich, the approaches suggested are described in a clockwise direction.

From Norwich

For travellers travelling by train from London, Norwich is one of the two best places to start, but it is a long way from any point on the walk. A variety of choices are possible.

1 Most of the trains from London connect with trains to Cromer or Sheringham from Norwich Thorpe Railway Station. This is probably best for those walking the Norfolk Way in the opposite direction to that described in this book. Those who have walked into Cromer can get a train back to Norwich; with one exception the local trains have a connection to London.

2 Buses 758 and 759 from Surrey Street bus station, Castle Meadow or Tombland for Cromer. This is a fast service and is recommended.

3 Bus 812 to Kenninghall (journey time 1 hour 15 minutes). From Kenninghall walk south-west along B1114 to Garboldisham (distance 6.5 km; 4 miles) and then turn right in Garboldisham village along the A1066 road (signposted Thetford). Almost the southern end of Peddars Way is reached after 7 km (4½ miles) walk to Boundary Plantation (TL/944830).

4 Bus 812 to East Harling (only three a day: journey time 1 hour 25 minutes). From bus stop in the market square walk north-west along B1111 road, following signs for Harling Road Railway Station. Go past the church and cross the River Thet. Here two choices are possible. Either turn left 100 metres after crossing the river and walk 3 km (2 miles) to Bridgham village and at village bus shelter turn right and then left on road to High Bridgham and Bridgham Heath where Peddars Way is reached at TL/935865; or walk 1 km (5/8 mile) to Roudham Turn and there turn left, following directions given under Harling Road Railway Station (below p.00).

5 Buses 814, 815, 816, 824, 826 and 834 to Watton. Either walk due west along B1108 road to Threxton and there join Peddars Way at TF/893000 or (on Wednesdays only at 12.15) catch bus 303 (indicated for Downham Market) from Watton to South Pickenham Hall Gates, retracing steps along B1077 road for 1 km (5/8 mile) to join Peddars Way where it crosses the road at

TF/867043. A co-operative bus driver may be prepared to allow the walker to alight at the point where the route crosses the main road.

6 Bus 834 (indicated for Watton) to Saham Toney. Alight in village, opposite village shop. Retrace steps along B1077 to church and village sign and there turn left along B1077. After 150 metres main road turns right; here keep straight on and follow minor road to Saham Hall. At crossroads opposite the lodge cottage (TF/891017), reached after 0.8 km ($\frac{1}{2}$ mile), walk west, to the north of Saham Hall. Peddars Way is reached after a further 0.6 km (3/8 mile) at TF/884018.

7 Bus 834 (indicated for Watton) to Ashill. Alight at village green, near village sign. Walk west past the church and along B1077 road for 2 km (1$\frac{1}{4}$ miles) to join Peddars Way where it crosses the road at TF/867043.

8 Bus 834 (indicated for Watton) to Holme Hale. Alight either at turn to village (TF/888071) or better at turning for North Pickenham (TF/887069) where road to Watton goes under the abutments of former railway bridge. Walk west along road for North Pickenham and Swaffham for 3.5 km (2$\frac{1}{4}$ miles) past Erneford House (on left at TF/874072) and over the railway to join Peddars Way at TF/855073, the abutments of a former railway bridge. There are signs for North Pickenham village at left-hand fork at TF/866074. Suitable for walk along original part of Peddars Way going north, either to A47 road or to Castle Acre.

9 Bus 434 (numbered 435 on Sundays) along A47. Alight where Peddars Way crosses the main road between East Dereham and Swaffham at TF/845095.

10 Buses 450, 451 (Saturdays only), 453 to Wells-next-the-Sea.

11 Buses 765, 766, 767 to Blakeney or Cley-next-the-Sea. Neither of the two last is recommended; the services are infrequent. Neither is a good way of returning to Norwich. Last bus back to Norwich from Wells is 14.15 and from Blakeney 13.30 (not Wednesdays); the late bus (18.40 on Wednesdays and Fridays; 19.32 on Saturdays) reaches Norwich long after the last train for London. In the summer the coast bus (service 417) reaches

Sheringham from Wells, Blakeney and Cley in time for the last
train with a London connection.

From Norwich there are a variety of access points for walking the
coast between Cromer and Great Yarmouth.

1 Bus or train to Cromer; see above.
2 Buses 731, 732, 734, 735 to Mundesley or Bacton. Alight at
   beach stop in either village.
3 Buses 724, 735 to Happisburgh. Alight either at the beach in
   Walcott or at Happisburgh church.
4 Bus 722 to Sea Palling. Alight at beach.
5 Bus 776 (summer Sundays only) to Sea Palling. Alight at beach.
   There are evening buses back to Norwich from Mundesley,
   Bacton and Happisburgh and one from Sea Palling to Wroxham
   with a connecting service to Norwich. On summer Sundays there
   are buses back from all these points, but no buses run on Sundays
   from either Sea Palling or Happisburgh between the last Sunday
   in September and the penultimate Sunday in May.

From Diss

There are several possible walks from Diss Railway Station, each
requiring most of a day. They can be recommended only to those
with a tent who carry a chemical toilet and who therefore could use
the Thorpe Farm camp site (TL/946841).

1 From the station approach, turn right on to the A1066 road,
   signposted Diss and town centre. It is possible to walk on a
   westerly course along the main road avoiding the town centre of
   Diss, by following the signs for Thetford. From Diss Railway
   Station there is a walk of 14 km (8¾ miles) to Garboldisham
   crossroads (TM/007815) and a further walk of 7 km (4½ miles) to
   Peddars Way at Boundary Plantation (TL/944833). This route
   has the disadvantage that the whole of it is on a main road along
   which vehicles drive very fast because there are very few bends.
   There are interesting places to visit on the way (see below).
2 Follow the directions above to Garboldisham crossroads, then
   walk 2.5 km (1¾ miles) to Riddlesworth crossroads (TL/980818)
   and there turn left. After 1.1 km (¾ mile) at Gasthorpe, following
   minor road, turn left and then right and cross River Little Ouse.

At crossroads in Knettishall (TL/973806) turn right along road
to Knettishall Heath. The start of Peddars Way is reached after 3
km (2 miles) at TL/944808.

3   There is also a walk along the Suffolk side of the River Waveney,
but this I have not tried. Follow the directions from Diss Railway
Station passing the mere. Then turn left to take the road over
Denmark Bridge and having crossed the River Waveney turn
right to head west along the ridge above the river. Keeping to
roads, the route goes through Redgrave Common, Thelnetham
and Hopton before reaching Knettishall.

Those taking the first of the routes from Diss will discover a number
of fascinating places along the A1066 road. Diss itself deserves to
be better known. The town is built north and east of Diss mere, a
six-acre pool beside the main road. It was so famous that a
sixteenth-century map had three places in England marked on it:
London, York and Diss, with the mere prominently shown. The
town retains many timber-framed buildings of late medieval and
Tudor date. The best is the former schoolhouse opposite the church.
Despite the Georgian and Victorian buildings in the town, the
overwhelming impression is of a much older town. None of the
eighteenth- and nineteenth-century buildings is particularly
assertive. The restrained character of the Corn Hall of 1854 sums
them all up. The church of St Mary retains much that is medieval:
the basic structure of tower, nave and aisles is fourteenth-century,
with a later clerestory.

At Roydon there is a twelfth-century church, partly extended by a
south aisle of a century later; the aisle was rebuilt in 1867. East of
Roydon is Bressingham. Here is kept the Bressingham Steam
Museum, whose exhibits include the locomotive *The Flying
Scotsman*. Bressingham church has a clerestory of the early
sixteenth century, donated by Sir Roger Pilkington. There are good
views across the River Waveney both at Roydon and at
Bressingham.

North of Bressingham, and part of the modern civil parish, is
Fersfield, where the Rev. Francis Blomefield was rector from 1729
to his death in 1752. Even before becoming rector, he was
collecting materials for his *History of Norfolk*, parts of which he

printed and published himself on a press set up in his stables. Much, however, remained uncompleted at his death: a second edition covering the whole county was published by the Rev. William Parkin in 1805. Blomefield collected information by circularising his fellow incumbents and by personal visits carried out on horseback.

West of Bressingham is South Lopham, a pleasant village which one might pass by without a further glance but for the church tower, one word describes it: stunning. The same word describes St Albans Abbey. The location is similar, on a prominent hill; the date is not dissimilar. Both towers belong to the first flush of Norman influence in England and both proclaim the message of domination. At South Lopham, the nave of St Andrew's church is Saxon, with one Saxon window surviving above a blocked north door, the latter of a more cosmopolitan style of the twelfth century built into the simpler Saxon stonework. The church is large, a living proof that on occasions the Saxon did build on the grand scale. The chancel and south aisle belong to the late fourteenth century: the former was given by Nicholas de Horton, rector from 1361 to 1380.

Gorboldisham village has many timber-framed houses, a fifteenth-century church and a windmill surviving 1.6 km (1 mile) to the south beside the B1111 road. West of the village beside the A1066 road is the Devil's Ditch, a linear earthwork facing west. It has been suggested that it is post-Roman. There are similar earthworks in northern Breckland, particularly the Launditch, which gives its name to Launditch Hundred. Between the Devil's Ditch and Garboldisham are a number of barrows, at present unexcavated but probably Bronze Age in date.

From Harling Road Railway Station

Not all trains from Ely to Norwich stop here, but those in the early morning to Norwich and those in the early evening from Norwich do. The station is particularly valuable to those leaving London on the 08.36 train from London Liverpool Street for Cambridge, Ely and King's Lynn, with a connection at Ely for Harling Road and Norwich. Those starting from Norwich can catch this train at Thetford by taking the 09.41 Norwich to Birmingham express,

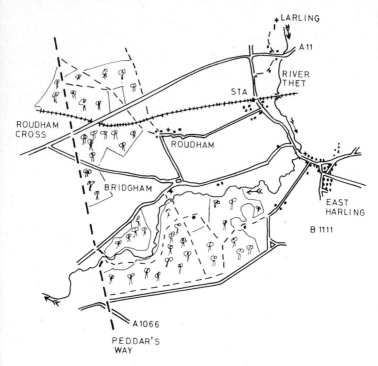

Routes from Harling Road railway station and East Harling to Peddars Way

alighting at Thetford and then retracing their journey to Harling
Road. To reach Peddars Way from Harling Road Railway Station
three walks are possible.

1 Turn north (i.e. left) from station and walk to the A11 road at
   Larling crossroads, approximately 1 km ($\frac{5}{8}$ mile). There turn left
   to walk south-west along the main road for 4.5 km ($2\frac{3}{4}$ miles) to
   where Roudham cross used to stand, at the crossing of Peddars
   Way and the A11 road. Peddars Way has long been marked by
   signs at TL/934871. For much of the route from Larling
   crossroads, the A11 road is dual carriageway, very straight and

used for very fast driving. This route to reach Peddars Way is not
recommended.

2 Turn south and across the railway tracks (i.e. right) from the
   eastbound platform of Harling Road Railway Station. Walk 150
   metres to Roudham Turn; turn right and walk 2.6 km (just over
   1½ miles) to Roudham village, passing Roudham Hall and the
   ruins of Roudham church. At the village crossroads either turn
   left along the metalled road for Bridgham village, reached after
   1.1 km (¾ mile), where turn right for High Bridgham and
   Bridgham Heath; or turn half left along farm track to High
   Bridgham and then turn left on the road to Bridgham Heath.
   Peddars Way is reached at TL/935865.

3 At Harling Road Railway Station, turn south and walk across the
   railway tracks, following directions for Roudham village as given
   in 2. At village crossroads go straight on from metalled road to
   farm track. This turns from a westerly direction to a
   north-westerly one after 200 metres. The railway is crossed at
   TL/939873 and the A11 at TL/947877. Either walk down the
   main road to Roudham Cross (TL/934871) or continue on farm
   track across field to a forest ride, turn left on to the forest ride
   and follow it for 1.2 km (¾ mile) to Peddars Way at TL/932883.

From any of these it is possible to walk to Threxton comfortably
within a day.

   Those walking from Harling Road Railway Station along either
of the walks 2 or 3 just described will pass through the village of
Roudham. The place is more a hamlet than a village. At the turning
from the road to East Harling there is a cottage built in the 1830s as
one of the lodges to Shadwell Park. Others exist in Brettenham
village, and in the centre of Roudham. Roudham Hall is a modest
early nineteenth-century house set beside the road. St Andrew's
church, Roudham is derelict and ivy-clad. It had been disused for
two centuries after the Reformation, but in the early eighteenth
century attempts were made to refurbish it. They came to nought
because the thatcher knocked his pipe out on his handiwork and the
whole roof was soon ablaze. After that the few parishioners did not
try again: some went to Bridgham, most as before used St

Ethelbert's, Larling. This is impressive when viewed across the fields. The south doorway is late Norman and there is other twelfth-century work in the dividing shaft of the piscina. The rest of the church is fourteenth-century, with a later tower. It is this which gives the church its strength when seen from afar.

From Larling

Larling crossroads (at TL/976889) is a stopping place, by request, on the long-distance buses from London to Norwich via Cambridge and Thetford. It is also on the route of the Bristol to Norwich bus. It is necessary to book in advance on these coaches. A co-operative driver may be prepared to allow the walker to alight at Roudham crossroads, 4.3 km (almost 3 miles) south-west of Larling crossroads.

Directions to reach Peddars Way, which crosses the A11 main road at Roudham crossroads (TL/934871) and is there marked by signs, are as given under Harling Road Railway Station. The A11 main road is not recommended as a walk.

From Thetford

Thetford is an interesting town in its own right (see below). There is a good train service from Birmingham, Nuneaton, Leicester and Peterborough; the last has connections from Yorkshire and north-east England. There are also trains from Ely connecting with trains from Cambridge and London, and express buses from London and Cambridge.

For all routes to Peddars Way, turn left on leaving the railway station signposted for town centre. The A11 road is reached after 300 metres. From the bus station, walk to the River Thet and along the riverside walk to the bridge. Turn right across bridge and walk up White Hart Street to the A11 road. From this point five routes are possible.

1 Turn left from the road from the station (right from White Hart Street) on to the A11 road and walk 7.5 km (4¾ miles) along main road to Peddars Way at Roudham Cross (TL/934871). This is not recommended.

2 Turn left on to A11 road and walk 2 km (1¾ miles) to turning on

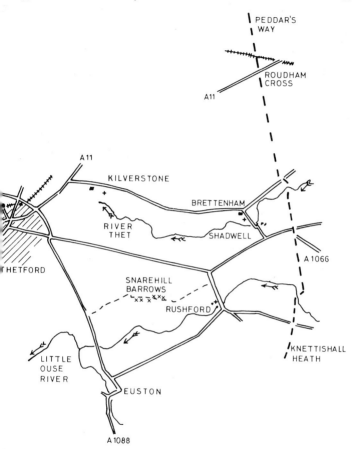

Routes from Thetford to Peddars Way

right from Kilverstone Hall and Brettenham. Here turn right and walk 5 km (3 miles) from Brettenham. After another 1.3 km (about 1 mile) walk along road to Bridgham, Peddars Way is

The bridge over the Little Ouse River at Thetford is built of cast iron. It was erected in 1829 and is the third oldest surviving iron bridge in England.

reached at TL/941844, just north of the crossing of the River Thet.

3 From road from station, cross A11 and walk into the town along White Hart Street, going past The Ancient House Museum. Turn left at Bell Corner, opposite the Bell Hotel and St Peter's church, and walk through pedestrian shopping area. From bus station turn right at Bell Corner and walk through pedestrian shopping area. At the Market Place, opposite the Town Hall, take the road dead ahead and walk along Castle Street to bridge over the River

Thet, following the A1066 road. From the bridge it is a walk of
6.7 km (4¼ miles) to Peddars Way at Boundary Plantation
(TL/944833).

4   Walk the 1.2 km (¾ mile) through Thetford to the bridge over the
River Thet as outlined in 3. Cross the bridge and follow the
A1066 road to junction with A1088 road. Turn right on to
A1088 road (signposted Ixworth and Bury St Edmunds). Take
extreme care when walking along main road as it is part of the
lorry route from Leeds to Harwich and Felixstowe. After 2 km
(1¼ miles) turn left at TL/890809 on to farm track through Great
Snarehill Belt. After 1.3 km (about 1 mile) the farm track forks.
Take the right-hand fork past the Seven Hills, a group of six
Bronze Age barrows surviving from the original eleven burial
mounds. After a walk of 3.5 km (2¼ miles) from the A1088 road,
the farm track ends at a metalled road in Rushford. Turn right
and south. After 600 metres cross the River Thet and then turn
left on to road to Knettishall Heath. Bear left at fork opposite
Rushford Hall (now a restaurant). The beginning of Peddars Way
is reached on Knettishall Heath at TL/944808.

5   Walk through Thetford and then along the A1088 road to
Euston, a distance of 4 km (2½ miles) from the bridge over the
River Thet. At TL/896794, 800 metres after crossing the River
Little Ouse into Suffolk, turn left along minor road lined with
trees through Rushford Belts. Rushford Hall is reached after 3.5
km (2¼ miles); Peddars Way on Knettishall Heath is a further 2
km (1¼ miles) further on. Directions from Rushford Hall are as
given in 4.

From Brandon

There is one long but good introductory walk from Brandon
Railway Station to Peddars Way. The Harling Drove Road, along
paths and metalled roads mainly through the forest, is 15 km (9½
miles) long. For those with a day to spare before walking the
Norfolk Way it is recommended, and for this reason it is described
in detail.

On alighting from the Ely train at Brandon Railway Station, cross
the railway by the footbridge and walk to the exit on the westbound

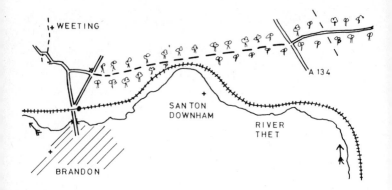

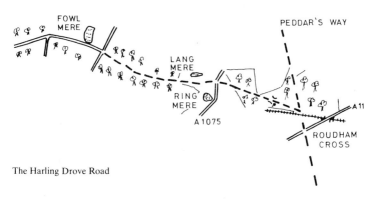

The Harling Drove Road

platform. At the end of the approach road beside the Great Eastern Hotel turn right to cross the railway tracks (level crossing). Turn half right to follow the A1065 road, signposted Swaffham and Fakenham. The town of Brandon is behind the walker; there are no shops between Brandon and Roudham Heath, so those wishing to buy supplies of chocolate, sweets, etc. should turn left at the Great Eastern Hotel and immediately cross the bridge over the River Little Ouse to walk into the main street of Brandon.

After crossing the level crossing over the railway tracks, walk along the A1065 road for 800 metres (½ mile) to crossroads formed by main road, a metalled road to the left and a track to the right at TL/788881. This is the entrance to the Harling Drove Road. There is a large barrow in the field to the left, just north of the metalled road.

Turn right from main road on to track and walk in an easterly direction for 5 km (3 miles) to junction with A134 road at TL/839888. The walk is at first uphill before descending to near the

Harling Drove Road goes through the woods north of Brandon and Santon Downham. These are commercial woodlands and trees are often left on the drove road to await marking before being taken to the woodyards beside Brandon railway station.

River Little Ouse and the railway line, north-west of Santon Downham. It then climbs again before a long descent. The whole of this portion of the Harling Drove Road is on a forest track.

At the junction with the A134, continue on easterly course for 3 km (2 miles) to New Buildings, the southern entry point to the Stanford Battle Ground Training Area, at TL/868894. Here the metalled road turns south of east, and goes past the picnic site at the Devil's Punchbowl and the large Breckland mere known as Fowl Mere. After New Buildings walk along the metalled road for 1.5 km (2 miles) to junction with metalled road running from south to north at TL/883892. This is about 300 metres east of Fowl Mere.

Fowl Mere is one of the Breckland meres. These are pools of stagnant water whose level is dependent on the water in the chalk below the surface. The Harling Drove Road passes others at Long Mere and Ring Mere.

From road junction at TL/883892 walk south-east along forest walk through Croxton Heath. After 1 km (5/8 mile) this turns to a more easterly direction and 1 km (5/8 mile) further on emerges from the forest to a heathland area. There are gates here. 800 metres after the gates the walk reaches the A1075 road. To the north of the track is Long Mere, and to the south Ring Mere. Ring Mere is one of two possible sites of the battle for Ringmer in 975; the other is Rymer in Suffolk, another Breckland mere. Both are the meeting-places for many parishes: seven at Ring Mere, nine at Rymer.

Ring Mere (TL/909878) is a nature reserve, at the centre of East Wretham Heath. It is managed by the Norfolk Naturalists' Trust.

From the A1075 road at TL/912883 follow the farm track which goes in an easterly direction across East Wretham Heath. This is between high grasses for 400 metres. It then becomes a walk through a plantation. After 1.5 km (1 mile) walk between the abutments of a former railway bridge at TL/925878. Peddars Way is reached at TL/933876, a walk of another 800 metres from the railway bridge abutments. The junction of the Harling Drove Road and Peddars Way is just north of the place where Peddars Way crosses the railway line from Thetford to Norwich and 400 metres north of Roudham crossroads.

Those who have walked from Brandon Railway Station along the Harling Drove Road should turn left to go north. After a walk of 3.2 km (about 2 miles) Stonebridge is reached. The walker may find accommodation at the 'Dog and Partridge' public house in Stonebridge at the end of a good day's walk.

From King's Lynn

For the traveller from London, King's Lynn is a possible starting point for walking the Norfolk Way, particularly the northern part of Peddars Way, or for reaching the Norfolk Coast Path. From the bus station there are several possible routes, essentially to Peddars Way.

1 Bus 434 (435 on Sundays) for Swaffham and Norwich. Alight between Swaffham and Necton where Peddars Way crosses the A47 road at TF/845095.

2 Buses 434, 435, 438 to Swaffham. Alight there and follow directions given under Swaffham below.

3 Bus 428 to Castle Acre (and Swaffham; some buses continue to Litcham and this may be marked on the indicator board). Alight at Loose's Stores, Castle Acre, just before road turns left to Newton-by-Castle Acre. The bus does not go into Castle Acre village. Alternatively ask the bus driver if you may be set down where the road from West Acre joins the Great Massingham to Castle Acre Road at TF/816157.

4 Bus 468 (has Cromer or Fakenham on indicator board). Ask to be set down where the Grimston to Great Massingham road crosses Peddars Way at TF/785221. This is before Great Massingham village and there are signs marking Peddars Way.

5 Bus 416 (for Wells). Alight slightly beyond Anmer crossroads at TF/754293 where Peddars Way crosses the B1153 road from Hillington to Great Bircham. Peddars Way is marked by signs. If the bus driver sets you down at Anmer crossroads, walk north-east following the bus for 300 metres to reach Peddars Way.

6 Buses 410, 411, 412, 413, 414, 417 to Hunstanton. Follow directions given under Hunstanton.

7 Bus 412 for Hunstanton via Sedgeford (about four a day). Alight at Snettisham Turn in Sedgeford. Take the left-hand fork in

Sedgeford village and walk east along B1454 road to Littleport
Farm (TF/723368). Peddars Way crosses the Docking to
Heacham road (numbered B1454) at Littleport Farm.

8 Bus 412 to Sedgeford, as in 7. Alight at Snettisham Turn in
   Sedgeford and walk east along B1454 road for 400 metres. There
   take the right-hand fork along minor road to Fring. This follows
   Heacham River. Peddars Way is reached after 2 km (1¼ miles) at
   TF/727356.

From Swaffham

Walkers who live in Nottingham, Leicester, Birmingham,
Manchester, Blackpool, Sheffield and places north and west of
these may find the easiest way to reach the Norfolk Way is by
long-distance bus. All the places mentioned have coaches either
daily or at weekends only during the summer months to either
Norwich or Great Yarmouth and Lowestoft. These services use the
A47 road between King's Lynn and Norwich. It is unlikely that an
unofficial setting-down point of Peddars Way at TF/845095 will be
established. However, Swaffham is a scheduled stopping place.
From the Market Place in Swaffham, a number of walks or buses to
Peddars Way are possible.

1 Walk east along A47 road past the churchyard of St Peter and St
   Paul parish church, Swaffham. Where A47 road turns left
   continue straight on along minor road to North Pickenham, going
   past wireless tower. Peddars Way is reached at TF/855073, a
   distance of 4 km (2½ miles). There turn left and north passing
   through abutments to former railway bridge.

2 Walk east along A47 road as in 1. At Wood Farm on minor road
   to North Pickenham, at TF/829086, turn left on to farm track
   and public footpath. This is 1 km (5/8 mile) from Swaffham town
   centre. After a walk of a further 1.8 km (about 1¼ miles) Peddars
   Way is reached at TF/847089. This crossing of tracks is known as
   Swaffham crossroads.

3 Walk east along A47 road to where Peddars Way crosses the
   main road at TF/845095. This is about 2.3 km (1½ miles), but it is
   not recommended.

4 Bus 434 (435 on Sundays) to where Peddars Way crosses the
   A47 road.

The market cross at Swaffham was erected in 1783 by the Earl of Orford. The statue on the top is of Ceres, the goddess of the plenteous fruits of the earth.

5 Bus 428 (indicated for Litcham) to Palgrave Turn, at TF/837108. The road to Palgrave Hall and Great Palgrave is on the line of Peddars Way.

6 Walk north from Swaffham Market Place along A1065 road for Fakenham. After 100 metres turn right on to road for Sporle. Follow this road for 2.7 km (almost 1¾ miles) to Palgrave Turn as in 5. Note the bus route in Swaffham is slightly different from this in the town.

7 Bus 428 to road junction at Bartholomew's Hills (TF/817131).

Alight here for crossing of modern route of Peddars Way across the Swaffham to Fakenham road (the A1065).

8 Walk due north from the Market Place in Swaffham along the A1065 road to Bartholomew's Hills (TF/817131), a distance of 4 km (2½ miles). This is not recommended, as the road is straight and taken by drivers at speed.

9 Bus 428 to Castle Acre. Alight at Loose's Stores, the Castle Acre village bus stop, or where the bus turns left for West Acre and East Walton, at TF/816157.

From Hunstanton

Directions for reaching the beginning of the Norfolk Coast Path are given in Part Three of this Guide. Those who wish to remain in Hunstanton all week and walk the coast path, travelling out each day, will find the summer only bus 417, which runs on Tuesdays, Wednesdays and Thursdays, valuable. It goes to Brancaster, Burnham Market, Overy Staithe, Holkham, Wells, Stiffkey, Blakeney, Cley-next-the-Sea, Salthouse, Sheringham and Cromer. A potential five-day schedule visit, using bus 418 on the Monday, is:

Sunday: Hunstanton to Brancaster
Monday: Brancaster to Wells-next-the-Sea
Tuesday: Wells-next-the-Sea to Blakeney or Cley-next-the-Sea
Wednesday: Cley-next-the-Sea to Sheringham or Cromer
Thursday: Sheringham to Cromer (if not done on the Wednesday)

The confident walker could probably walk the Norfolk Coast Path in three days, leaving a day free to walk Peddars Way north from either Castle Acre (TF/816157) or Grimstone Heath (TF/785221), having arrived at either place by bus from Hunstanton to King's Lynn and then another bus out from King's Lynn. Walking south from Holme-next-the-Sea to take a bus from there into King's Lynn is not recommended, as bus connections can be uncertain.

From Wells-next-the-Sea

Wells-next-the-Sea is a better centre than Hunstanton to walk the Norfolk Coast Path, again using bus 417 with bus 418 on Mondays and Fridays. It is not especially suitable for walking Peddars Way.

From Blakeney or Cley-next-the-Sea

Either Blakeney or Cley-next-the-Sea is a possible centre from which to walk the Norfolk Coast Path. The disadvantage is that bus 417 is restricted in the days on which it operates.

From Sheringham

Sheringham is a popular small holiday resort on the route of the Norfolk Coast Path. From the bus stop outside the Railway Station several services run to points along the coast which can be used for beginning a day's walk.

1 Bus 417 to Hunstanton, Wells-next-the-Sea, Blakeney or Cley-next-the-Sea on Tuesdays, Wednesdays, and Thursdays in the summer.
2 Bus 780 to Wells-next-the-Sea, Blakeney or Cley-next-the-Sea on Tuesdays, Wednesdays, and Thursdays in the summer.
3 Bus 768 to Holt for bus 774, Tuesdays only, to Blakeney.
4 Bus 774 to Cley-next-the-Sea, on Tuesdays and Wednesdays only.
5 Bus 775 to Cley-next-the-Sea and Blakeney, on Fridays only.
6 Buses 468, 768, 769 (summer only) to Cromer, frequent daily service.

From Cromer

Cromer is a possible centre to walk either the Norfolk Coast Path or the walk from Cromer to Great Yarmouth. Bus services with connections exist along the coast in both directions.

1 Bus 417 (summer only) to Hunstanton, Wells-next-the-Sea, Blakeney or Cley-next-the-Sea, runs on Tuesdays, Wednesdays and Thursdays only.
2 Bus 780 (summer only) to Wells-next-the-Sea, Blakeney or Cley-next-the-Sea, on Tuesdays, Wednesdays and Thursdays only.
3 Buses 774, 775 to Cley-next-the-Sea and Blakeney as noted under Sheringham.
4 Buses 468, 768, 769 (summer only) to Sheringham.
5 Bus 768 to Overstrand and Mundesley.
6 Buses 778, 779 to North Walsham, for connections with services

731, 732, 735 to Mundesley, Bacton, Happisburgh. Note there are no suitable ways of using this connection to return to Cromer in the evening.
7 Buses 778, 779 to Stalham, for connections with service 722 to Sea Palling and 724 to Happisburgh. There are no suitable connections back by this route to Cromer, except via Norwich.
8 Bus 780 (summer only) to Mundesley, Bacton, Happisburgh, Sea Palling, Winterton, Hemsby, Caister-on-Sea and Great Yarmouth. Runs on Tuesdays, Wednesdays and Thursdays.

Part Two: Peddars Way

Peddars Way is the Roman road from Colchester to the Wash. Only the Norfolk portion is well preserved and this forms the basis of the first section of the Norfolk Way. It runs from Knettishall Heath in Suffolk across country to Holme-next-the-Sea on the north Norfolk coast.

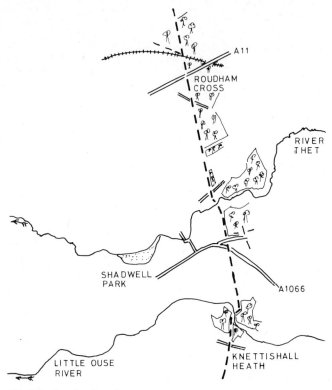

A11

ROUDHAM
CROSS

RIVER
THET

SHADWELL
PARK

A1066

LITTLE OUSE
RIVER

KNETTISHALL
HEATH

Knettishall Heath to Roudham Cross

1 Knettishall Heath to Roudham Cross
6.7 km/4¼ miles

The opening section of Peddars Way from Knettishall Heath to
Roudham Cross will ultimately follow a path along the original
route of the Roman road. However, this must await the opening of
the Countryside Commission route and the building of bridges over
the River Little Ouse at Rushford and over the River Thet at
Brettenham. The component parts of the route can already be
walked, if with a little difficulty of initial access. The route which
follows is based on the proposed Countryside Commission route
and on the assumption that bridges will be provided. It is illegal, and
fairly dangerous, to cross the river except by bridges.

Peddars Way begins on the western edge of Knettishall Heath. If
you have followed either the Snarehill walk or the Rushford Belts
walk from Thetford, turn right at the beginning of the heath and
walk about 300 metres uphill beside the heath for what remains of
the Suffolk portion of the route south to Colchester.

For the main walk of Peddars Way north to Hunstanton, turn left
if you have come from Thetford or right if you have come from Diss
and walked the full length of Knettishall Heath. The first 700
metres (almost ½ mile) are a forest walk and will lead to a bridge
over the River Little Ouse. Originally there was a ford here. Cross
the bridge and follow the route on a north-easterly course for 200
metres before turning left, i.e. north. The walk now follows the edge
of a belt of trees for 1.4 km (almost 1 mile) before reaching the
A1066 main road. Cross this, carrying straight on, climbing the
bank and walking 200 metres along the former main road, now a
Norfolk County Council Highways Department depot. It is not
private land and there is sufficient path to avoid the heaps of gravel,
tar and other road-mending materials. At the end of this, the walker
should cross the road leading to East Harling and follow the path
along the edge of the plantations. Peddars Way is very distinct as
the raised agger planted with trees along the very edge of Boundary
Plantation. In 1979, this was marked off by fences and quite

Peddars Way begins with a descending path on Knettishall Heath, south of the Little Ouse River in Suffolk.

impassable. Walkers are advised to follow the path immediately to the right of this. After 800 metres ($\frac{1}{2}$ mile) this comes to the River Thet. The stones of a former ford here were not removed until after the Second World War. A new bridge is to be built across the river to take Peddars Way on its northward course.

After crossing the bridge, the walker has a straight walk northwards for 3 km (2 miles) to Roudham Cross, which used to stand where Peddars Way crosses the main A11 (London to Norwich) road. The route goes uphill from the crossing of the River

Thet and the first 1.6 km (1 mile) was restored by the Countryside Commission in 1978–81. After crossing the river, the first noticeable feature is four fine birch trees, standing rather isolated beside the path, which then crosses the Brettenham to Bridgham road. There is a gap in the hedge here indicating Peddars Way, opposite a long narrow coppice on the line of the Roman road. Walk uphill towards this and skirt round it on the right of the trees, keeping the wood to the left. After leaving the coppice behind strike out northwards to the end of the next patch of woodland, and walk through the woodland for 400 metres. The path is overgrown in places. The path now comes to Brettenham Heath, leaving the woodland after a green gate. It rises sharply for 300 metres before crossing the minor road from Bridgham, where those who have walked from Harling Road Railway Station would join Peddars Way. A walk of 600 metres along the edge of woodland takes the walker to the main A11 road where Roudham Cross used to stand.

Until the designation of the Countryside Commission comes into force, crossing the rivers presents problems in walking the direct route. Over the River Little Ouse crossings exist at Rushford, at TL/924812, and at the eastern end of Knettishall Heath, at TL/956807. There are crossings over the River Thet at Shadwell, at TL/933832, and at Bridgham, at TL/957856. All four crossings are some distance from Peddars Way, and their use distinctly represents a second best.

From Knettishall Heath there is an eastern walk, along the road through the heath to the crossroads beside the camp site. Here turn left and walk along the road over the River Little Ouse, carrying straight on to where the road bears right. Continue straight on along a farm track to the A1066 road, turning left on to the main road. At the bend follow Peddars Way to the River Thet and the Thorpe Woodlands camp site. Here turn right and follow the marked path, first east and then north-east, which leads through the woodland to an unmetalled road and bridleway going south to north. Turn left (i.e. north) and walk to the bridge over the River Thet. After crossing the bridge, turn right along the road for Bridgham village, and in the village turn left and left again to walk along the road past High Bridgham to join Peddars Way on Bridgham Heath.

Alternatively, after crossing the bridge over the River Thet, turn left (i.e. south-west) and walk towards Brettenham. After 1.9 km (1¼ miles) turn left through the gap in the hedge opposite the four birch trees between the road and the River Little Ouse, to join Peddars Way, walking the 3 km (2 miles) to Roudham Cross, along the original route of Peddars Way.

A western walk using the crossings at Rushford and Shadwell has much less connection with the original route of Peddars Way and is entirely on roads. Walk west from Knettishall Heath for almost 2 km (1¼ miles) and then just after Rushford Hall turn right to cross the River Little Ouse. In Rushford, at the fork opposite the school, bear right and then at the A1066 turn right to walk north-west for 1.3 km (¾ mile). At the turning for Shadwell and Brettenham turn right, descending to the River Thet, and walk past Brettenham church to the Kilverstone to Bridgham road. Here turn right. After 1.3 km (¾ mile), the original route of Peddars Way is reached; after a further 2.5 km (1½ miles) the walker comes to Bridgham village. One can either walk north from the birch trees or along the road to High Bridgham and Bridgham Heath to reach Peddars Way.

It is hoped that by the time this book is published the directions for alternative routes will be superfluous. However, they are useful as pointers to interesting places on either side of the route of Peddars Way.

The remains of All Saints' church, Knettishall, are 3 km (2 miles) east of the beginning of Peddars Way. The church is disused but the west tower, under construction in the 1450s when money was left for its building, remains. St Peter's, Riddlesworth, contains the fittings which were brought there from Knettishall church, including a Jacobean pulpit, fifteenth-century panels painted with St Peter and St Edmund from a screen, and the royal arms of Charles I painted in 1632 but refurbished in 1666 (both dates are clearly visible). The church is beside Riddlesworth Hall, built in 1900. Both are best approached by turning south from the A1066 at TL/967820.

On both Knettishall Heath and Rushford Heath there are various barrows, presumed to be of Bronze Age date.

Walking from Thetford to Knettishall Heath, the walker will have

The Romans built a ford for Peddars Way to cross the River Thet east of Brettenham. The stones of the ford remain under the shaded area on the left on the photograph. Peddars Way comes into the photograph, bottom right. In the background is a staunch connected with a former watermill at the nearby Thorpe Farm.

passed Rushford Hall, now a restaurant. It is a rather fine seven-bay house of about 1700. Rushford Hall is south of the Little Ouse River; the village, church and former college are north of the river. It is a very attractive small hamlet, with the school set between the junction of two roads. The church dates to 1342 when Edmund Gonville, rector of Shadwell and Rushford since 1326, founded a college of a master and four fellows. This able man, who had been steward to Earl de Warenne and then to the Earl of Leicester in the same year as he founded Rushford College, became Rector of Terrington and Commissioner of the Marshlands of Norfolk. When taxed in 1346, his position was comparable to that of the Prior of Norwich, the Abbot of St Albans or the Bishop of Hereford. In 1348, Edmund Gonville founded Gonville Hall, Cambridge, refounded by another Norfolk man, John Caius, in 1557 and now known as Gonville and Caius College.

Rushford church is large but is not now as long as when it was built. Its style recalls the beginning rather than the middle of the fourteenth century. South of the church are the former college buildings, long since turned into a private house. It was designed round a court and only the north and west ranges survive. The north façade is heavily restored.

Shadwell Park is on the south side of the River Thet. The house (not open to the public) is a vast Victorian monstrosity which somehow just about comes off in its combination of finicky detail and heavy structure. S.S. Teulon was the architect. He also built the lodges with tree-trunk verandas and the red-brick farm labourers' houses to be found in Brettenham village to the north of the River Thet. Brettenham church retains a Norman doorway but is otherwise a restoration by Teulon of 1852.

Bridgham is very much a contrast. Here no dominant squire held sway. The church lost its tower a long time ago and despite its length does not seem over-large in its substantial churchyard. There are two fonts: a Norman one from Roudham and a fifteenth-century one on two steps.

Walking along the road to High Bridgham there are good views across the valley of the River Thet, with the trees of Harling Plantations to the south.

The villages of East Harling, Middle Harling and West Harling are somewhat off the route of Peddars Way, lying to the east of it. Those arriving at Harling Road Railway Station may well, however, visit one or more of them. East Harling is the largest of the villages and in the early Victorian years was regarded as a small market town. There are still many urban features such as an auctioneer's, a small market held in the square and a larger than normal complement of shops. The town has both timber-framed and brick houses round the square and in the village street. The church of St Peter and St Paul is away from the village at its western end, overlooking the River Thet but 7 metres above it. Viewed from afar, either from a railway train or when approaching the village from the station, the church looks spectacular without being grandiose. The spire and its buttresses seem to set off the width and the length of this major church. Internally, it owes much to successive owners of Harling Manor. The Harling family contributed to the south chapel a monument of a knight and his lady of the late fourteenth century, now combined with the tomb of Sir Robert Harling (died 1435). Sir Robert's daughter, Anne Harling, had two husbands: Sir William Chamberlain (died 1462) and Sir Robert Wingfield (died 1480). Much of the fifteenth-century stonework and fenestration was financed by them. Sir William has a chantry between the chancel and the north chapel: one of those unexpected pieces of funerary sculpture sometimes encountered in an almost unknown church. Sir Robert Wingfield's memorial is the great east window. It retains its original glass with scenes from the Annunciation to Pentecost. The sixteenth century saw the manor pass to the Lovell family, who built a great mansion in the fields near to the church. Sir Thomas Lovell died in 1524. In the church, serving as his memorial, is a copy of the bronze medallion by the Florentine, Pietro Torrigiano, which once adorned the great house but is now in the King Henry VII chapel at Westminster Abbey close to one of Torrigiano's other works; the tomb of the king's mother, Lady Margaret Beaufort, whose chancellor Lovell was. It is a reflection on his standing and his wealth that a Norfolk knight could commission the same expensive foreign artist as the king. Sir Thomas's son and grandson, Sir Francis Lovell (died 1551) and Sir Thomas Lovell (died 1567), have very plain memorials above the sanctujry, one to the north, the other to the south. The last of the family, Sir Thomas Lovell (died 1604), and his wife have a great alabaster pair of effigies recumbent on a tomb chest within columns and iron railings: one of the heaviest Jacobean pieces in Norfolk. East Harling church is worth visiting to experience how the English ruling class treated the village church: a radical might suggest it was with contempt. The changing fashions in funerary sculpture are neatly chronicled at East Harling. There are other interesting pieces, too, in the church, particularly the screens which divide off part of the south aisle to form a south chapel.

Information

DISTANCE	6.7 km/4¼ miles
STATIONS	Harling Road, Thetford
BUSES	none
REFRESHMENTS	Rushford Hall restaurant
SHOPS	Thetford, Bridgham, East Harling
BANKS	Thetford, East Harling
ACCOMMODATION	East Harling
CAMPING	Thorpe Woodlands (chemical toilet required)

2 Roudham Cross to Threxton
15.6 km/9½ miles

Roudham Cross at TL/934871 is where Peddars Way crosses the main London to Norwich road, the A11. It is conveniently 400 metres south of the junction of Peddars Way and the Harling Drove Road from Brandon Railway Station and 650 metres north of the minor road from Bridgham village to Peddars Way. Roudham Cross is thus conveniently sited for those whose walk along Peddars Way has begun either with a walk east from Brandon Railway Station or a walk west from Harling Road Railway Station (see Part One).

From Roudham Cross to Threxton, Peddars Way follows the original route for 11.3 km (5½ miles) before deviating from a straight course going north-north-west. Thereafter, it follows a new path round Merton Park on its western side to reach existing paths which take Peddars Way to its junction with the B1108 road from Watton to Bodney. The distance from Roudham Cross to Threxton by the fully established route is 15.6 km (7½ miles), but until the route west of Merton Park is made safe from residual shells a detour going round the south, east and north sides of the park and through the village at Merton is necessary. The distance is 16.5 km (8¼ miles) by the route east of the park.

At Roudham Cross take great care in crossing the main A11 road. The road is extremely straight between Thetford and Attleborough and at Roudham Cross the main road is dual carriageway. Motor traffic between Kilverstone and Larling often goes at speeds exceeding 90 k.p.h. (58 m.p.h.).

The route of Peddars Way from Roudham Cross goes slightly west of north for 3.5 km (2 miles) along a rising track with a sandy surface. After 350 metres take great care in crossing the main Norwich to Ely railway. Except for trains which have just stopped at Harling Road Railway Station train speeds, in particular those of the Norwich to Birmingham express, tend to be high on this stretch of line.

Almost immediately north of the railway crossing is the Harling

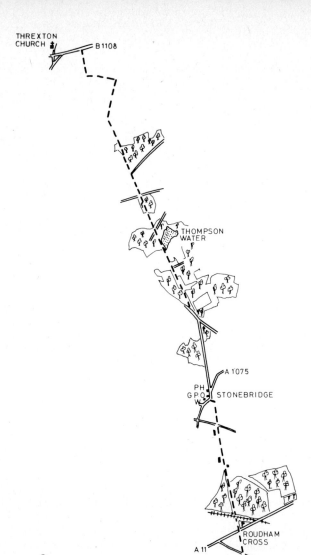

THREXTON
CHURCH

B 1108

THOMPSON
WATER

A 1075

PH
GPO STONEBRIDGE
W

ROUDHAM
CROSS

A 11

2

Roudham Cross to Threxton

Drove Road on the left. Those wishing to visit the nature reserve on East Wretham Heath should turn left here and walk in a north-westerly direction for 2.5 km (about 1½ miles) to reach the nature reserve including Lang Mere and Ring Mere (description in Part One). Those continuing along Peddars Way should follow the rising ground. At about 1.8 km (1¼ miles) north of Roudham Cross, the line of the former railway from Roudham Junction Halt to Watton and Swaffham is seen on the left. Large buildings of pig and poultry farming can be seen west of this. On the right at the same point is a service installation of the natural gas pipeline from Bacton on the north Norfolk coast to the south midlands (see Part Four for notice of the gas terminal). The route of Peddars Way is to the east of the railway for 1.7 km (1 mile) and straight. After crossing a minor road it goes downhill for 600 metres and then turns left to go under the former railway. Only the abutments of the bridge survive, and as the walker emerges from between them the remains of a former windmill can be seen dead ahead. Beyond this at TL/915906 is East Wretham church, dedicated to St Ethelbert, basically a Victorian structure of 1865 with some representative Victorian stained glass and reused Norman stonework.

After turning left under the former railway bridge, the walker immediately turns right on to the A1075 road which after 150 metres takes him into the centre of Stonebridge, one of the hamlets of East Wretham. This is a good place to stop for lunch, as there is no other convenient village before Threxton. Stonebridge has both a village shop and a good pub, the 'Dog and Partridge'.

Those with time to spare while walking Peddars Way could spend a day in the northern part of Breckland, staying at the 'Dog and Partridge' Inn at Stonebridge. This would enable the walker to visit the pretty village of Great Hockham (around TL/953924). The church, dedicated to the Holy Trinity, is of the fourteenth century, with contemporary wall paintings. There is no tower. The church is reached by a marked path at the western end of the village. The former village school, now the village hall, lies on the southern side of the village green, which has a large tree in the centre. The houses are of the fifteenth century and later, the older ones being timber-framed.

North of Roudham Cross, Peddars Way begins a long ascent through the trees on Roudham Heath. In the middle ground is the Norwich to Ely railway line. The Harling Drove Road joins Peddars Way just to the north of the crossing keeper's cottage.

Further afield is Breckles, a decayed village. Breckles Hall is an Elizabethan house built for a recusant family, the Woodhouses. It has a genuine priest's hole, where a Catholic priest to serve the family and others in the area could be hidden. In the late sixteenth century many of the leading gentry families in Breckland remained adherents to the old faith. The Anglican church of St Margaret at Breckles, at TL/972057, has Saxon work, as does the church of Rockland All Saints, at TL/994960. The tower at Breckles is pre-Norman, with a particularly good tower arch. At Rockland, the nave is the oldest surviving part of the building; its corners have large slabs set alternately upright and horizontally in a fashion known as long-and-short work. Opposite to the church of Rockland All Saints is the stark ruin of the two halves of the tower of the church of Rockland St Andrew, set in an overgrown churchyard. The small brick building in the south-east corner of the churchyard of Rockland All Saints is a Victorian schoolroom, now disused.

There is a fine uphill walk along the tree-lined road between Mount Pleasant (at TL/993949) and Shropham village crossroads (TL/985932). Shropham church is large; it was the chief church of a deanery in the middle ages. Essentially a thirteenth-century structure, it has a very fine roof. Visible from the churchyard is the eighteenth-century rectory. Shropham also has many orchards. A walk round these, possibly also taking in the mere at Stow Bedon (about TL/950965) and the isolated, basically Victorian, church of St Botolph, at TL/962957, which serves Stow Bedon village, makes an excellent introduction to northern Breckland.

Just north of the pub in Stonebridge there is a fork in the road. Peddars Way takes the left-hand fork along a metalled road for 2.2 km ($1\frac{1}{2}$ miles) which goes uphill for much of the distance. The fork for Peddars Way is well marked at Stonebridge, as is the main road on the right for Great Hockham.

From Stonebridge to Galley Hill, Peddars Way follows a metalled road. After 600 metres the route is wooded on the left; after 800 metres ($\frac{1}{2}$ mile), it is wooded on the right also. To the left was Wretham Park. The house designed by Sir Reginald Blomfield has been demolished and the former church of St Lawrence is a ruin beside Wretham Hall Farm. The latter is one of the farms still working inside the Stanford Battle Training Ground which is immediately west of Peddars Way for the whole distance between Stonebridge and Threxton.

It cannot be emphasised too strongly that under no circumstances should the walker stray into the Stanford Battle Training Ground. His one step may be his last.

In the middle of Wretham Park is Mickle Mere (at TL/908917) which, like Fowl Mere, Long Mere and Ring Mere, all elsewhere in the modern Wretham parish, is a Breckland mere, a large pool

Dutch elm disease has wrought havoc with trees alongside parts of Peddars Way. These trees were photographed in 1979 near Stonebridge.

whose level is dependent on the level of water retained in the chalk below ground and not on the rainfall. Special permission must be obtained by anyone wishing to visit Mickle Mere and applications must be made in advance in writing to the military authorities.

Mickle Mere is west of the metalled road which is the original route of Peddars Way as it ascends Woodcock Hill. The wood on the left is known as Brickkiln Covert, one of the frequent reminders of this area of how long-established brick building has been in northern Breckland and the adjacent Fenland area of Norfolk. In the next section of the walk along Peddars Way, the walker may take a detour to visit the early-sixteenth-century Great Cressingham Priory.

At Galley Hill, TL/923927, the road from Stonebridge is joined by one from Great Hockham. Here the walker should veer left and descend the hill ahead. About 200 metres beyond this road junction, the walker reaches the foot of Galley Hill. The metalled road appears to go straight ahead, continuing on a north-westerly course. It originally went to the village of Tottington, which because of the battle area has been completely deserted since 1942. At the foot of the hill, at TL/922929, there is a wide opening on the right, which appears to be for a cart track and heads north-north-west through trees. This is the route of Peddars Way. In 1980 it was not well marked.

The walker should walk along this track for 4 km (2½ miles). There are a number of tracks to the east, on the walker's right, as he goes north. To the west is the Stanford Battle Training Ground. This is marked off by waist-high fences, and there are large red notices warning about unexploded shells. Do not ignore these.

The walker is quite safe as long as he remains on the path.

After walking along the track for 2 km (1¼ miles), the walker crosses the River Wissey. About 1850 the river was damned and allowed to flood, producing a large lake, Thompson Water. Stanford Water, inside the Stanford Battle Training Ground, is also an artificial creation. Extremely good coarse fishing is to be had on Thompson Water, and from June to March the walker will often see anglers practising their sport. It is also a noted local beauty spot. On the short stretch north of Thompson Water and the portion through Shakers' Furze north of this, the walker should beware of cars, as the route is not closed to motor traffic. There is a road to Thompson village at TL/912952, and Bronze Age round barrows are visible just within the Stanford Battle Training Ground. The barrows are among the trees of the aptly named Madhouse Plantation, which lies west of Peddars Way and also east of it, to the north of Thompson Water.

Thompson village is worth visiting. The church is fourteenth-century and built of knapped flint. Surprisingly, there are no aisles. Part of the screen contemporary with the building of the church survives, as does a wealth of Jacobean woodwork: pulpit, reader's desk, benches and a family pew. Contemporary with the church was Thompson College, founded in 1349 for a master and five priests to serve the chantry chapel of St Martin in the parish church. The buildings are now represented by some fourteenth-century windows in College Farm, at TL/933967.

After Madhouse Plantation, Peddars Way passes through an area of heathland, but it is still enclosed within fences separating walkers from the army ranges. North of this the route passes through Shakers' Furze, a belt of woodland, before crossing a road with an entry to the Stanford Battle Training Ground on the walker's left. Thereafter the route is along a fenced footpath through open ground going up hill to Sparrow Hill.

At Sparrow Hill, TL/905966, the walker has two choices. The route designated by the Countryside Commission will take him round the western edge of Merton Park. In June 1982, this was cleared of unexploded shells and made safe through the efforts of a group organised by Lord Walsingham, the owner of Merton Park. There are still many red notices warning of the dangers and although the route has been made safe, some walkers may prefer to take the detour round the eastern side of Merton Park.

This involves the walker in turning right from Peddars Way at the Sparrow Hill entrance to the Stanford Battle Training Ground. The walker should walk for 1.3 km (¾ mile) along a metalled road to a T-junction in the road, there turning left along the eastern edge of Merton Park. After 1 km (⅝ mile), turn left at the crossroads beyond Merton Park for Merton village. Here walk straight on through the village green, with council houses on the left. The road becomes a cart track beyond the houses and continues for 1.2 km (¾ mile) in an west-north-west direction, becoming westerly. It then turns right and continues for a further 750 metres (about ½ mile) to the B1108 road, at a point 800 metres (½ mile) east of Threxton church.

The Countryside Commission route takes the walker along the western edge of Merton Park. At Sparrow Hill, go straight on in a northerly direction, following the path which largely follows the

Many stretches of Peddars Way pass between low banks on either side. This is a typical stretch of the walk near to Merton Park.

Merton parish boundary for 1.6 km (1 mile). Thereafter walk north along an unmetalled road for 1 km (5/8 mile), passing the buildings of Home Farm on the left. At a crossing of tracks turn left along an unmetalled road and bridleway. After another 750 metres (about $\frac{1}{2}$ mile) the track turns right and a further 750 metres ahead reaches the B1108 road, at a point 800 metres ($\frac{1}{2}$ mile) east of Threxton church.

Here the walker can either continue the route of Peddars Way or turn right for Watton. A walk of 2.5 km ($1\frac{1}{2}$ miles) will take him into the town, where accommodation can be found.

Merton means 'mere town' but all that remains of the mere now is a lake in front of the shell of Merton Hall. The house was largely burnt out in a fire in 1956 and of the original Jacobean house only the gatehouse remains. The surviving part of the house is the work of Edmund Blore, a much underrated early nineteenth-century architect, who added a wing in the same style as the body of the house. The park also houses St Peter's church, of which the tower and adjacent west wall are Saxon and the rest a fine example of early fourteenth-century work. The interior contains both Jacobean and Stuart woodwork. There is a brass to William de Grey, who died about 1495; he is shown with his two wives and numerous progeny. Merton village has some timber-framed houses and includes the site of a moated farmstead, at TL/907987.

Watton is a minor market town which comes to life on a Wednesday when the market is held in the town street, but on Thursday afternoons (early closing day) is extremely quiet. Apart from one modern housing estate south of the town, which includes a large school, and some developments to the north, Watton is a single-street town. Notable buildings are a large former brewery, now a photographer's workshop, and the Clock Tower. This was set up in 1679 to commemorate the rebuilding of Watton after a disastrous fire on Saturday 25 April 1673 which destroyed sixty houses and the butchers' shambles (or market stalls). Damage was estimated at £10,110. Most of the town's surviving buildings belong to a later rebuilding, a century or so after the fire, and many have shop fronts inserted in their ground floors. The population of Watton doubled in the early nineteenth century and the church of St Mary is largely a rebuilding of 1840 designed to accommodate the greatly increased number of parishioners. Much of the stonework was reused by the early Victorians, who retained the Norman tower and the thirteenth-century chancel. The church is east of the town, close to where the former railway line crossed the B1108 road from Watton to Norwich. Beyond this road is Carbrooke, where there is a large airbase.

South of Watton, beside the A1075 road from the town to Thetford, is Wayland Wood. Here the story of the 'Babes in the

Wood' is reputed to have originated. The wicked uncle lived at nearby Griston Hall. Those who take a bus from Norwich to Watton via Wymondham and Attleborough will pass the wood.

Information

DISTANCE	15.6 km/9½ miles
STATION	Harling Road
BUSES	East Harling, Watton
NATURE RESERVE	East Wretham Heath
REFRESHMENTS	Stonebridge, Watton
SHOPS	Stonebridge, Great Hockham, Watton
BANKS	East Harling, Watton
ACCOMMODATION	East Harling, Watton

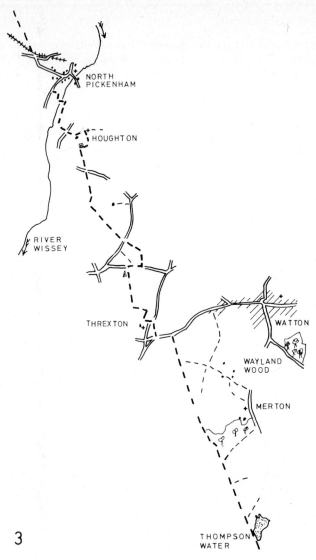

NORTH
PICKENHAM

HOUGHTON

RIVER
WISSEY

THREXTON

WATTON

WAYLAND
WOOD

MERTON

THOMPSON
WATER

3

Threxton to North Pickenham – a suggested route

3 Threxton to North Pickenham
11 km/7 miles

Of all the sections of the Norfolk Way, the portion of Peddars Way from Threxton to North Pickenham is the most difficult to describe. The original line of the Roman road has been almost totally obliterated. No parish boundaries form straight lines which can be taken to represent a lost portion of Peddars Way. There is some possibility that the drive of Saham Hall and a minor track from west of Ashill to Uphall Grange may represent original portions of the route of Peddars Way: these seem to continue the line of the path from Merton Park to Threxton. The track to Uphall Grange serves as the parish boundary of Ashill and North Pickenham and was originally the parish boundary of Houghton-on-the-Hill and Ashill.

Given that the Countryside Commission route has yet to be agreed, and at present is not easily walked, it seems worth while to describe a more practical route from Threxton to North Pickenham.

All routes, including that suggested by the Countryside Commission, begin by turning left at the B1108 road off the path from Merton Park. Those who have found accommodation in Watton should walk west out of the town for 2.8 km (1½ miles) to rejoin Peddars Way at Threxton. When the Countryside Commission route is established, there will be a path above the road. Until then, face the oncoming traffic and walk west for 800 metres (½ mile). After 500 metres, the Countryside Commission route and other suggested routes for Peddars Way between Threxton and North Pickenham diverge. The Countryside Commission route will be described later.

On Threxton Hill, turn right, i.e. north, from the main road and descend the steep road down to Threxton church. All Saints' church is of thirteenth-century date but restoration in 1865 revealed a Saxon nave 6.4 metres (21 feet) wide, which is wider than the surviving Saxon nave of South Lopham church.

From Threxton church there are two ways to North Pickenham. The first is to walk round the farmyard next to the church and head

Threxton church has Saxon origins, but was enlarged at the beginning of the thirteenth century. The round tower is earlier. It was added in the middle decades of the twelfth century.

north-west along a footpath to Limekiln Farm. On reaching the metalled road beyond the farm turn right and walk north, subsequently veering to north-north-west for 3.2 km (2 miles) to the crossroads by Hall Farm, South Pickenham. Cross the B1077 road and walk along the minor road on the east side of the River Wissey which veers round to north-east, passing the turn to Houghton Farm after 1.2 km (¾ mile). After 2.3 km (1½ miles) turn left on the road to North Pickenham village.

The alternative is to walk north-north-west along the road from
Threxton church, passing Saham Hall on the left after 1.4 km
(almost 1 mile). Saham Hall is a minor early nineteenth-century
house in a late Georgian style with a farm attached. The drive
probably preserves a piece of the original Peddars Way. At the
crossroads just beyond Saham Hall, marked by a house on the
right-hand corner dead ahead, turn left and walk west for 2 km (1¼
miles), along the road to Great Cressingham. Great Cressingham is
about 3 km (2 miles) to the west. This village is famed for its church
of St Michael and for a house known as Great Cressingham Priory.
The church has a fine frieze of carved panels with crowned swords
and crowned Ms (representing St Michael). The roof is alternating
hammer-beams and arched braces, akin to the great roofs of the
Fens, such as St George's church, Methwold. Great Cressingham
Priory, 200 metres north of the church, is a great house of which the
east range survives. The south part has the upper room externally
panelled in brick; the ground floor is plain, although the present
façade may have been altered from the mid-sixteenth-century
original. The much longer northern section of the range is timber
framed. At Methwold, 14 km (9 miles) to the south-west, the
former vicarage has a decorated brick gable to an otherwise
timber-framed house. Great houses were often showy on their
public front but much more utilitarian on the other ranges: the
classic example is the great gatehouse of Oxburgh Hall of 1482,
only 10 km (6 miles) west of Great Cressingham.

At the crossroads reached after a walk of 2 km (1¼ miles) from
Saham Hall, those not wishing to visit Great Cressingham should
turn right to head north along a metalled road. This is narrow, has
much grass growing in the centre and is used by the army on
manoeuvres. Walkers should look out for military vehicles in
convoy driving at speed.

The walk is 2.8 km (1¾ miles) to the junction with the B1077 road
at Hall Farm, South Pickenham. There are good views of South
Pickenham Hall on the left. It looks early nineteenth-century in
date but this is deceptive. The house was rebuilt in its original style
in 1904 and reuses many of the old materials, including much of the
decorative brickwork. Cross the main road and walk north, then

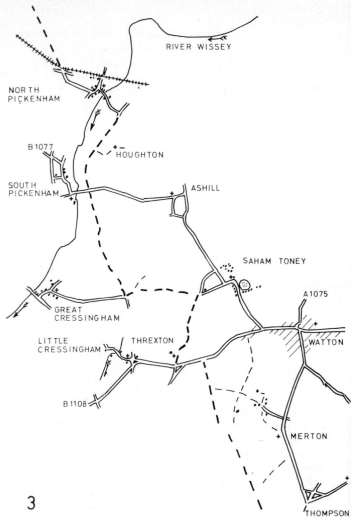

RIVER WISSEY

NORTH
PICKENHAM

B 1077

HOUGHTON

SOUTH
PICKENHAM

ASHILL

SAHAM TONEY

A 1075

GREAT
CRESSINGHAM

LITTLE
CRESSINGHAM

THREXTON

WATTON

B 1108

MERTON

3

THOMPSON

Threxton to North Pickenham – projected final route

north-west along a metalled way to a turning into North Pickenham village. Turn left after 2.3 km (1½ miles) on to this road.

There is another alternative route heading north-east to Ashill from the crossroads west of Saham Hall, but between Ashill and Uphall Grange part of this route may not be on a public right of way. The first part follows a public road, which ultimately goes due north. At a fork in the road after 1.5 km (1 mile) turn left, and then after 300 metres follow the road northwards to the B1077 road, crossing the road to walk along the path to Uphall Grange. Beyond the farm, the path turns left and then after 400 metres turns right to revert to a northerly course. After 400 metres the path turns left again to head north-west and descends to the road above the east bank of the River Wissey. Turn right at the road and then after 300 metres turn left to walk into North Pickenham village.

This route skirts the interesting villages of Saham Toney, Ashill and South Pickenham. Saham Toney is a 'mere' village with a great sheet of water in the village centre. The micro-climate is totally different beside the pool from what it is beside the church 200 metres to the north. There is a pleasant green with the village sign in front of the church. St George's church is large, basically of thirteenth-century date but with a later tower. This has a frieze commemorating the dedicatee and the Virgin; the west door is surrounded by stonework with the dragon facing his tormentor. There is a large red brick Georgian rectory adjacent to the church.

Ashill is famed as the village of the goose. The bird dominates the twentieth-century village sign. The glebe is devoted to orchards; the village is away from the church and is set round a large square green flanked by modest houses. St Nicholas's church is fourteenth-century with later, over-restored fenestration. Ashill church is 500 métres east of the route suggested above; the village is a further 500 metres to the north-east.

About 2.4 km (1½ miles) west of this route, and 500 metres west of Hall Farm on the B1077, is South Pickenham. There are good views of Pickenham Hall from the first route described, but this large Edwardian house is seen from the rear: the main front faces west. The church was partly rebuilt at the same time. It includes an organ case in High Victorian style, said to be by Pugin and made for

Augustus Sutton, Rector of West Tofts in the third quarter of the nineteenth century. The village is interesting as a late example of an estate village.

The route proposed by the Countryside Commission is more complex than either of those just described, which sometimes take the walker along roads, but unfrequented ones. The main danger on the first alternative suggested is from army vehicles using the road south from South Pickenham. Otherwise all one is likely to meet is isolated farm vehicles.

The Countryside Commission route from Threxton to North Pickenham involves walking on the road north from Threxton church and then, after crossing a minor stream, bearing left along a path beside the edge of a field. Thereafter the path follows the edges of fields, turning right, then left, then right to head north for 1.2 km ($\frac{3}{4}$ mile) to the road from Saham Toney to Great Cressingham. Here it turns right to go east along the road for 500 metres, then left to head in a north-easterly direction for 4 km ($2\frac{1}{2}$ miles) to Houghton Farm. At a coppice to the south of the farm, the route turns right, then left and then left again to go round the farm and take the track westwards descending to the River Wissey, and crossing the road before turning north to go alongside the river to a new bridge south of North Pickenham village. On crossing the river, the proposed route skirts fields to reach the road from South Pickenham to North Pickenham. At the village it turns left and after 600 metres follows the road where it bears north-east. North Pickenham railway bridge is ahead, just the other side of the road from Holme Hale to Swaffham.

The main advantage of the proposed route is that it takes the walker close to the disused church of St Mary, Houghton-on-the-Hill, which is covered in ivy, stands inside a dense thicket of undergrowth, and is not particularly exciting. Saxon windows are visible internally, but even those most enthusiastic about Saxon churches might not think this worth the effort.

The route proposed by the Countryside Commission approaches North Pickenham from a different direction from those suggested earlier. These both enter the village from the south-east, crossing the River Wissey on the road bridge. North Pickenham church (St

Andrew's) is seen to the north and on the right. The church is largely Victorian with contemporary stained glass. Beside the church is a contemporary village school. Church and school form an attractive group. At the T-junction just beyond the church, the walker should bear left and follow the road south through the village. This turns west-north-west and after 600 metres bears right to head north-west. North Pickenham railway bridge is seen ahead, beyond the Holme Hale to Swaffham road. The bridge has been dismantled, but the jambs remain. The line ran from Thetford to Watton and Swaffham, and was closed in 1964. The masts of the television booster station can be seen ahead and on the left when walking from North Pickenham.

Information

DISTANCE	11 km/7 miles
STATIONS	none
BUSES	Watton, South Pickenham, Saham Toney, Ashill, Holme Hale, Swaffham
REFRESHMENTS	Watton, Ashill
SHOPS	Watton, Saham Toney, Ashill, North Pickenham, Swaffham
BANKS	Watton, Swaffham
ACCOMMODATION	Watton, Swaffham

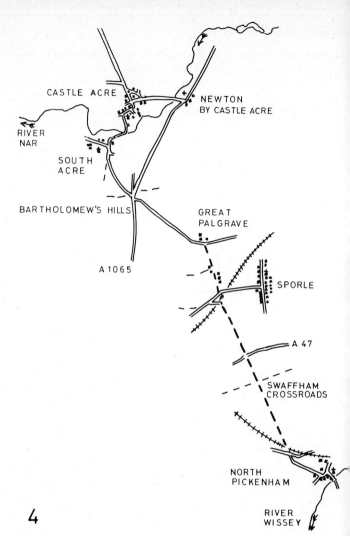

CASTLE ACRE

NEWTON
BY CASTLE ACRE

RIVER
NAR

SOUTH
ACRE

BARTHOLOMEW'S HILLS

GREAT
PALGRAVE

A 1065

SPORLE

A 47

SWAFFHAM
CROSSROADS

NORTH
PICKENHAM

RIVER
WISSEY

4

North Pickenham to Castle Acre

4 North Pickenham to Castle Acre
10.7 km/6¾ miles

From the railway bridge at North Pickenham to Great Palgrave, Peddars Way follows its original course for 5.5 km (3½ miles). Thereafter, to Castle Acre, the route takes the most convenient and the most picturesque of the existing roads and tracks.

At the railway bridge beyond North Pickenham, Peddars Way can be seen stretching ahead, going under the railway bridge and north-east. Take this track, which is straight on from the road from North Pickenham village which the walker has hitherto followed. For 2.3 km (1½ miles) the route is along a wide track, lined with a low hedge including trees. There are interesting fungi growing on the side of Peddars Way here and on trees in the hedge. On this portion the ground is often wet and slippery. Good views of the countryside of northern Breckland are to be seen to the right, i.e. eastwards.

After 1.7 km (1 mile) the walker reaches a crossroads of Peddars Way and a track running from east to west. This is known as Swaffham crossroads. To the west is the town of Swaffham; to the east can be seen the tower of Necton church (All Saints'). This church, at TF/878097, has one of the finest hammer-beam roofs in Norfolk and a splendid pulpit given in 1636. On top of the tall tower is a lantern, copying that at Shipdham church, 8 km (5 miles) to the east. Shipdham church, at TF/957075, has a whole range of seventeenth-century fittings: commandment board and royal arms, in the north aisle and nave respectively, resited from their original tympanic setting in the chancel arch; a pulpit, and a lantern spike. Another feature is the immense braces to the north aisle. To reach Necton, turn right at Swaffham crossroads on Peddars Way and walk east for 1.2 km (¾ mile), then turn left, i.e. north, and walk to the A47 main road. Turn right on to the main road and walk for 2 km (1¼ miles) to the turning for Necton.

Those who wish to visit Swaffham from Peddars Way have a much less traffic-infested route. Turning left, i.e. westwards, at

A particularly good stretch of walk begins at the old railway bridge at North Pickenham. The track and the supports for the railway line were dismantled after the Watton to Swaffham trains were withdrawn in 1964, but the bridge piers remain.

Swaffham crossroads there is a walk of 1.9 km (1¼ miles) to Wood Farm. Here bear right on to a metalled road which leads to the eastern end of Swaffham, carrying straight on and then following the road round when reaching the A47 main road.

Swaffham is an elegant town. Not for nothing was it known as 'the Montpellier of England'. The market place is a large triangle formed by the junction of the Brandon to Fakenham road (the A1065) and a branch therefrom to King's Lynn (now part of the

Fungi have taken root at several places along the edge of Peddars Way. This large mushroom can be seen growing on a tree stump near to Swaffham Crossroads, on Peddars Way to the south of the A47 trunk road.

A47). A subsidiary element is the road to East Dereham and Norwich (now the A47). Like the A11, the A47 is a creation of the turnpike commissioners of the eighteenth century: the medieval road from King's Lynn to Norwich ran far to the north. It crossed Peddars Way at the southern end of Massingham Heath and proceeded through Litcham, Mileham, Brisley and North Elmham before following the modern A1067 down the Wensum valley.

In the centre of the market place is the market cross, a rotunda erected in 1783 by the Earl of Orford with a figure of Ceres on top of the dome. This is the best place to stand and survey Swaffham. To the south, houses on both sides of the market place stretch away to form London Street, and the great funnel narrows to the width of an ordinary street in something over 100 metres. The buildings here lack any hint of pretentiousness. The finest houses are north-west of the market cross, on the west side of the market place. Most are good, provincial Georgian houses of the pleasing variety which gives a place an air of distinction. The School House and adjacent Headmaster's House are dated 1736; Oakley House is a little later. There is a little infilling on an island north of the market cross. The buildings are a hotch-potch and include the very old, such as a fifteenth-century timber-framed house, the not so old, such as the Assembly Room of 1817 and the former Corn Exchange of 1858, and some recent additions which do not seem out of place. Perhaps it would take more than the bulldozers and the juggernauts to ruin Swaffham. Sir Nikolas Pevsner thought the Victorians did their best to do so with the Corn Exchange and the Baptist Chapel, also of 1858: the first he describes as 'depressing', the second as 'terrible'. The latter is one of those vast, cavernous nonconformist chapels which speak volumes about the kind of faith they embodied: strong on hope, weak on charity.

Much more a joy to behold is the parish church of St Peter and St Paul. The churchyard stands high above the road to Norwich, but the west end is approached only by an alley through buildings. The church is long, as befits a prosperous town church; the prosperity is that of the late fifteenth century. Above the nave with its clerestory of thirteen lights is a hammer-beam roof, one of the most splendid in Norfolk. The rector who rebuilt the chancel died in 1474; John Chapman paid for the north aisle in 1462 and financed the rebuilding of the tower in 1507–10. With him is connected the legend of the pedlar's dream, of the man who was directed to go to London. The man dreamt that if he stood on London Bridge he would meet a man who would tell him something to his advantage. In the dream the man stood on London Bridge and was approached by another who told him to go home to Swaffham where he would find wealth by digging in the pedlar's garden under a pear tree. John

Sporle church has a thirteenth-century tower. The upper part with the battlements was added in the fifteenth century.

Chapman is reputed to have thanked the stranger and gone home to Swaffham. He dug as directed and found two pots of gold.

Returning to Peddars Way: the walk north from Swaffham crossroads reaches the main A47 road after 600 metres. Cars and heavy lorries bound from Birmingham to Great Yarmouth can be seen ahead along most of the rising approach. Cross the main road with care and carry straight on along a metalled farm road for 1.4 km (almost 1 mile) before turning left when the road turns to cross the former railway line from Swaffham to East Dereham. After 100

Between Palgrave Hall and Great Palgrave, Peddars Way is used as a bridleway and farm road. The farm in the background is the remnant of the deserted village of Great Palgrave.

metres turn right and just before this road crosses the old railway line turn left for Palgrave. There is a bus shelter at this turn.

The road to Palgrave is part metalled and partly a grassy track. Follow this for 1.2 km ($\frac{3}{4}$ mile), passing Palgrave Hall after 600 metres. Here Peddars Way bears slightly to the right; do not take the direct right-hand turn. The stretch from Palgrave Hall to Great Palgrave is narrow and is used by vehicles.

Palgrave is one of the many deserted villages of Norfolk.

Earthworks are visible in the fields to the east of Great Palgrave
Farm. Today the three farms of Palgrave Hall, Great Palgrave and
Little Palgrave are all included in the civil parish of Sporle with
Palgrave. Sporle village is reached from Great Palgrave by turning
right, and from Palgrave Turn (at TF/838109) by continuing
straight on rather than turning left to continue on Peddars Way.
Sporle is one of the most attractive villages in Norfolk, with a small
stream running down the side of the village street. Houses on the
western side of the street are approached by small bridges over the
stream. The church of St Mary, which overlooks a small village
green, essentially dates to the thirteenth century. There is a camping
site in Sporle.

From Great Palgrave, the route of Peddars Way is an artificial
one. The original route headed north to Little Palgrave Hall and
thence over Hungry Hill into Castle Acre, probably along the road
which goes from east of Little Palgrave Hall to Castle Acre. Those
wishing to walk this way should turn right at Great Palgrave and
then after 1.2 km (¾ mile) turn left, i.e. north, at the telephone box
at the northern end of Sporle village. After 1.6 km (1 mile) turn
right at the crossroads and then after 300 metres bear right along a
metalled track. Follow this road for 2 km (1¼ miles), crossing the
main A1065 road after 1.3 km (¾ mile). From Hungry Hill, and the
main road, the route descends steeply to the valley of the River Nar.
There is a bridge across the river outside Castle Acre. On crossing
the bridge, turn right and then left to ascend through the village,
passing under the Bailey Gate to Stocks Green with Castle Acre
village sign.

The route favoured by the Countryside Commission for this
section of Peddars Way involved turning left, i.e. north-west, at
Great Palgrave and walking along this road for 2 km (1¼ miles) to
the ancient road junction at Bartholomew's Hills. Part of this is to
be along a specially constructed path on the right-hand, i.e.
northern, side of the road. The descent is fairly steep to approach
the main A1065 road. Cross the main road with care: it is almost
straight, and is treated as a race track by some motorists. The
official route of Peddars Way follows the road signposted to South
Acre, which is straight on from the road from Great Palgrave, but

An eighteenth-century tombstone in the churchyard at South Acre.

after 50 metres it bears right and then climbs for 800 metres ($\frac{1}{2}$ mile) before turning right to reach a crossroads. At the crossroads continue straight on for Castle Acre and descend to the River Nar. South Acre village is reached by taking the left-hand fork at the crossroads. The road to Castle Acre turns right after 200 metres to run above the River Nar for 300 metres. There are good views of Castle Acre Priory from the bank above this road, and from the stepping stones across the River Nar. Cross the river by the stepping stones and then turn left with the road. 200 metres beyond the river there is a right-hand turning. One can either take this and turn left after 400 metres to climb through Castle Acre village passing under the Bailey Gate to arrive at Stocks Green, or continue straight on at

The Bailey Gate at Castle Acre overlooks Stocks Green, the modern centre of the village. There are grooves for a portcullis within the arch at the back of the gate. The two round towers face north and date to the thirteenth century.

The complex of buildings erected in the sixteenth century as the Prior's Lodging at Castle Acre Priory was later used for the bailiff's house for the Coke estates in this and adjacent parishes. This single building has a variety of materials used in its construction. The oriel window and the gable above are of dressed stone with brick used in the steps of the gable. The walls beside the oriel window are rubble masonry, but these stand on flint walls. In the porch there is dressed stone flanking the entrance, with flint and dressed stone chequerwork as a decorative bank between the arch and the window. Beside the window is flint with above this timber-framing infilled with plaster. Parts of the side walls of the porch are brick.

the turning, climbing the steep road between high banks with St James's church on the right. At the top of the climb, beside the north-west corner of the churchyard, turn right to walk 200 metres into Castle Acre village, arriving opposite the Bailey Gate on Stocks Green.

Describing the complexities of the route has resulted in the interest of both Bartholomew's Hills and South Acre being left aside. At Bartholomew's Hills, where the route crossed the A1065 road, no fewer than six roads now meet and originally there was a seventh. A field has now taken the place of the Fincham Drove Road from the south-west. The Fincham Drove can be traced across Norfolk to the Fens and is Roman in origin. A long portion of it forms the northern part of the parish boundary of Swaffham, which has as its eastern boundary the route of Peddars Way between North Pickenham railway bridge and the railway bridge at Palgrave Turn. From the A1065 road between Hungry Hill and Newton-by-Castle Acre, good views of Castle Acre castle with the church and priory beyond can be obtained.

A visit to South Acre can be rewarding. The village is west of Peddars Way and is approached by turning left at the crossroads after Bartholomew's Hills. There is a fine brick house, of seventeenth-century date, opposite the church and several interesting cottages elsewhere. The church itself has a complex architectural history, beginning in the thirteenth century and continuing with various rebuildings to the eve of the Reformation, with the tower probably the last to be rebuilt. The north chapel, beside the chancel, is the earliest surviving portion of St George's church. Here various lords of the manor have been buried: Sir John Harsick and his wife, Lady Joan Harsick, hold hands in their fine brass of late fourteenth-century date (he died in 1384), and one of the best Jacobean monuments in Norfolk was erected in 1623, during his lifetime, for Sir Edward Barkham. The plain Norman font has a sixteenth-century font cover. In the churchyard are several eighteenth-century tombstones.

The road through South Acre continues west to the River Nar, which it crosses by a deep ford. Views of what remains of the Augustinian priory at West Acre can be seen from here. The gatehouse is on the village green at West Acre, which is a village built mostly of flint and brick. One yeoman's house, of the sixteenth century, is clapboarded and built in an imported style under a single roof with the outer bays jettied.

Castle Acre takes its name from the vast castle earthworks on the eastern side of the village, but the site is older than this. Peddars Way was a Roman road and some form of small Romano-British settlement may have existed where the road crossed the River Nar. Certainly the crossing was considered an important one, for in the late fourth century a group of Saxons seems to have been induced to come to defend the crossing as part of an organised settlement of Germans in late Roman Britain. They buried their dead in the most westerly field of the parish, and this cemetery spread over into West Acre. Discoveries of Saxon cremation urns have been made at various times since 1857; most are now in Norwich Castle Museum, but others are in King's Lynn Museum. The compact village of Castle Acre is above the most obvious crossing point of the river, and in its present form is probably no earlier than the eleventh century, which is the date of the castle earthworks. These earthworks comprise a castle mound, or motte, formed from a small natural hill which has been protected from the bank of the bailey by a deep and wide ditch on the northern and western sides, an inner bailey to the south of the motte, and a large outer bailey west of the inner bailey in which much of the village of Castle Acre has been built. The castle was in existence in 1086 when it was recorded in Domesday Book. On the motte was built first a square keep, presumably very much like those surviving at Castle Rising and at Norwich, and then a large, open circular shell keep whose overall diameter was 50 metres (160 feet), making it among the largest of its kind in England. For comparison, Restormel Castle, Cornwall, is only two-thirds of that size, though it is of similar date to the surviving buildings at Castle Acre. The best indication of the date of building of the present stonework at Castle Acre comes from the Bailey Gate facing Stocks Green which gave access to the outer bailey of the castle. This is thirteenth-century work with half-round towers facing Stocks Green and a high arch between them; it retains fittings for a portcullis. Originally there was a similar gateway in the south bank of the castle earthworks facing the River Nar, but this had been demolished before the nineteenth century.

Contemporary with the original building of the castle is William de Warenne's foundation of Castle Acre Priory, established in 1190 as a daughter house of the Priory of St Pancras at Lewes but soon

The south-west tower of the church of Castle Acre Priory retains the decorative arches of its twelfth-century construction but the robbed walls of the church on the right have lost virtually all trace of the decoration which once covered their exterior. Some indication of the vertical strips and the round arches both of the north cloister walk and between the windows can still be seen on the south wall of the church. The Prior's Lodging is on the right and the photograph was taken looking along the west cloister walk.

made independent. The Norman family of de Warenne were also Earls of Sussex and held Lewes Castle. Of Castle Acre Priory an impressive amount remains, despite the dissolution of 1537 and the subsequent quarrying of the stonework for building materials. The priory is west of the village, approached by a lane leading west from

Stocks Green at the end of which the walker turns left. The first
building one sees is an early Tudor brick and stone gatehouse: a
presage of the early sixteenth-century opulence of the Prior's
Lodging, south of the great west front. This is Norman, the only part
of the early church standing to anything approaching the full height
for more than a single arch, and very solid, having originally only
narrow lights to relieve the heavy vertical stress of the blind
arcading. In the fifteenth century a great west window was inserted,
but alterations to the plan of the church were confined to the
eastern end. Here the five apses of transepts, aisles and choir were
squared off and replaced with a presbytery added to the eastern end
in work beginning in the fourteenth century. It was never quite
completed, for the south transept retains its apse: the others are
marked by lines of gravel in the grass laid out by the Ancient
Monuments Inspectorate of what is now the Department of the
Environment; when in 1929 the Earl of Leicester gave Castle Acre
Priory to the nation it was the Office of Works. By then, what
remained of the church, apart from the west front, was a much
mutilated north wall, most of the north and south transepts and
some of the piers from the great tower which originally stood at the
crossing space. Of the west towers, that to the south has survived to
the height of the west front, but little remains of the northern one.

West and south of the south-west tower is the Prior's Lodging,
incorporating the west range of the twelfth-century cloister. This
area has the most extensive alterations in the whole priory, having
been enlarged more than once. First to be built was an elaborate
porch in the centre of the range, with a chamber above; this late
twelfth-century structure has now been enclosed within the brick
and flint outer porch of the early sixteenth century. In the
fourteenth century, the original prior's apartments in the northern
bays of the western range had been extended westwards to provide
a vaulted cellar and a study for the prior. This building stands at
right angles to the west front as one approaches the priory and is the
first building the visitor sees. Today, there are big sixteenth-century
windows including a large elliptical bay facing north and a square
bay facing west. Much of the good preservation is due to its
subsequent use as the bailiff's house for the Coke estates in Castle

Acre from the sixteenth century onwards.

Rather less use could be made of the other claustral buildings. On the south of the cloister, all that is left of the frater, or refectory, is two low walls. Neither the original kitchen to the west of this nor its fifteenth-century replacement built on a bridge over a drain from the rere-dorter, or washing place, is well preserved, although four central pillars of the twelfth-century kitchen suggest a stone louvre, or chimney, above a central hearth. East of the later kitchen is the rere-dorter, preserving twelve lavatory seats, parts of the side walls of the range 27.75 metres (91 feet) long, and both gable ends. North of the rere-dorter and forming the east range to the cloister garth was the dormitory, built in the mid-twelfth century and given external buttresses on its eastern side in the early fourteenth century. Except for the roof and floor joists this is largely complete, with a row of pillars down the centre of the lower floor originally meant to take vaults. The monks slept on the upper floor and the stairs survive. Between the dormitory and the south transept was the chapter house, built in the twelfth century with an eastern apse replaced by a large flat window in the fourteenth century. Most of the detail has been robbed from the chapter house. Robbed almost to their foundations are the two halls of the infirmary, east of the dormitory; the northern hall was built with the majority of the claustral buildings in the twelfth century, the southern one is a fourteenth-century addition.

The village of Castle Acre is between the castle and the priory. At the eastern end is St James's church, whose independent existence meant that unlike Binham Priory or Wymondham Abbey the church of Castle Acre Priory did not continue after the Reformation as the parish church of the village. The present church is an impressive, fifteenth-century structure which largely reuses work of two hundred years earlier. It is long and high, with a west tower above the clerestory. Inside there is much late medieval woodwork: screens separating nave from chancel and small chapels from the rest of the aisles, pulpit retaining the original paintings of Latin doctors, seats, benches and misericords and a font cover whose condition suggests some mutilation. Only the roofs are modern.

Just as the priory reflects Norman piety and Tudor opulence, the parish church suggests late medieval wealth and Victorian poverty. Castle Acre, despite its being part of the Coke estate, was not a closed village. Many lived here who worked elsewhere and the village reflects the open nature of its society a hundred years ago. Around Stocks Green, the houses are little flint cottages, some now incorporating various shops and including most of the village pubs. On Bailey Street the façades have been rendered, but the side walls are still flint: much of the stone had been robbed from castle and priory. Today, priory, castle and parish church bring an influx of visitors in high summer; in autumn, spring and winter a different air pertains and the visitor can have the monuments to himself.

Information

DISTANCE	10.7 km/6¾ miles
STATIONS	none
BUSES	Holme Hale, Swaffham, Necton, the A47 main road, Palgrave, Castle Acre
ADMISSIONS	Castle Acre Priory; Castle Acre castle: both standard Department of the Environment hours (see above)
REFRESHMENTS	Swaffham, Necton, Castle Acre
SHOPS	North Pickenham, Necton, Swaffham, Sporle, Castle Acre
BANKS	Swaffham
ACCOMMODATION	Swaffham, Castle Acre
CAMPING	Sporle, Castle Acre

5 Castle Acre to Anmer
15.2 km/9¼ miles

From Castle Acre to where it crosses the B1153 road near Anmer, Peddars Way is an almost straight track, following the line of the original Roman road across Norfolk. In places the original construction of the raised agger of the Roman road can be clearly discerned, as can the banks and drainage ditches either side. North of the original line of the A148 main road from King's Lynn to Fakenham and Cromer, Peddars Way serves as a parish boundary for 9.3 km (about 6 miles) with Harpley, the Birchams and Fring on the eastern side and to the west Flitcham-cum-Appleton, Anmer, Dersingham, Shernborne and Snettisham. The junction of Peddars Way with another Roman road, that from Gayton to Brisley, serves as a marker for a parish boundary. The west to east road forms the southern boundary of the parishes of Great Massingham and Rougham, and the northern boundary of West Acre and Castle Acre. Where Peddars Way crosses this road, later incorporated in the medieval road from King's Lynn to Norwich, the parishes of West Acre and Castle Acre meet. Their joint boundary follows a generally southerly direction to the River Nar.

The village of Castle Acre is north of the River Nar. The walker wishing to follow Peddars Way northwards can conveniently begin on Castle Acre Green, standing outside the Bailey Gate, beside the village sign. From there walk 100 metres east to where the metalled road turns left, and here turn left along it. After a further 50 metres, the walker will come to a crossroads on the opposite left-hand corner of which is a shop called Loose's Stores. The Castle Acre village bus stop is here, as buses on route 428 do not go into the village but, having come from King's Lynn, turn left on the road to Newton-by-Castle Acre. This road is to the walker's right as he faces north.

Newton is not really a village, having only two farms, a few houses, and a superb church, All Saints'. This is one of the many Saxon churches of this part of Norfolk. Except for the east wall of

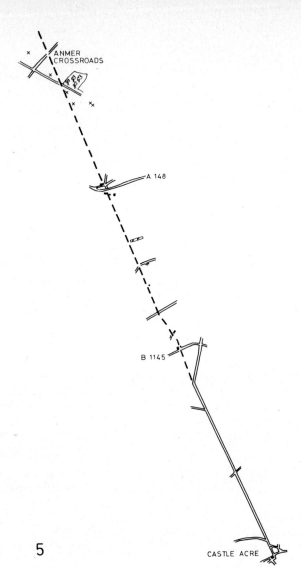

ANMER
CROSSROADS

A 148

B 1145

CASTLE ACRE

5

Castle Acre to Anmer

St Mary's church, Gayton Thorpe, has a Saxon tower to which was added a final stage in the twelfth century. Unusually for a village church, there are porches to both the north and south doors.

the chancel and the roofs (which are modern) the whole structure dates from the eleventh century. The church is unusual among Saxon churches with a central tower. At nearby Great Dunham, the lower walls of the tower are continuous with those of the nave and the chancel arch is the eastern arch of the tower. At Newton-by-Castle Acre, the walls of the tower are continuous with those of the chancel and the nave is appreciably wider than the tower and the chancel, with the chancel arch usually placed at the western arch of the tower. The central tower once stood above a crossing space, and both on the northern side and more explicitly to the south the former roof lines and edges from removed walls can be seen.

The churchyard at Newton-by-Castle Acre is large and occupies a considerable space above the River Nar. Higher up the river valley are the small villages of West Lexham and East Lexham. East Lexham church (St Andrew's) has some fourteenth-century stalls, probably reused from Castle Acre Priory, inside its chancel, which has a typical Victorian stained glass window. The fabric is probably late twelfth-century, but the tower with its bell openings in the uppermost stage is Saxon. Lexham Hall is an eighteenth-century structure. The River Nar has been diverted and widened to provide a suitable view beyond the terrace.

A circular tour based on Castle Acre, walking from there eastwards to Newton-by-Castle Acre, thence along the main A1065 road to West Lexham and thereafter by minor roads to East Lexham, Great Dunham and Sporle before returning along the route of Peddars Way through Great Palgrave and South Acre to Castle Acre, would take a day. As with other suggestions made in this guide, it depends on the time available to the walker.

The walker who cannot spare a day for this walk will press on northwards from Castle Acre. From the shop at the crossroads there is a path on the left-hand side of the road, to where the road from Castle Acre to King's Lynn goes off to the left. Thereafter for 4.8 km (about 3 miles), the walker has to walk along the fast, straight track of the road from Castle Acre to Great Massingham until it diverts from the line of Peddars Way at Shepherd's Bush (TF/795201). When the Countryside Commission has completed the designation of the Norfolk Way, there will be a footpath along

North of Castle Acre, Peddars Way becomes increasingly solitary. The photograph shows where it crosses a farm track in the vicinity of Great Massingham.

the right-hand side of the road, but only for part of the way. Until then, the walker must observe the rule of the road and walk facing oncoming traffic. If two or more walkers are together single file is recommended.

Between the village of Castle Acre and Shepherd's Bush, the road crosses two roads only. The first (at TF/807176) at Old Wicken Farm is reached after walking 2 km (1¼ miles); the second is a further 2 km (1¼ miles) on from this, and is where the Roman road

A corner of the village of Great Massingham, to the east of Peddars Way. The village pond can be seen in the left foreground and the Methodist chapel is the building on the extreme right.

from Gayton to Brisley crosses Peddars Way. Beyond this point, the walker is in the parish of Great Massingham for 4 km (2½ miles). If he wishes to visit Gayton, the village is reached after a walk of 8 km (5 miles) to the west, partly along the Roman road and partly along the B1145 road. Gayton when approached from the east is dominated by the tower of a derelict windmill. Milling is still a major business in the village. The church of St Nicholas is fourteenth-century and large for a village church in this part of

Norfolk. South-east of Gayton is the small hamlet of Gayton
Thorpe. The church there has a Saxon tower but the rest was rebuilt
in the fifteenth century. The nave roof is contemporary with the
rebuilding, as is the Seven Sacrament font. On Gayton Thorpe
Common, south-west of the hamlet and south of Gayton village, a
Roman villa is known to exist. Excavated in the 1920s, it revealed
traces of second- and third-century occupation, including a
tesselated pavement. North-east of Gayton village is Eastgate
House County Home; built in 1836, it was originally the workhouse
of the Freebridge Lynn Poor Law Union. North of Gayton, the next
village is Grimston, famed for its fine pots, especially jugs with faces
moulded on to them, made in the thirteenth and fourteenth
centuries. A hamlet of Grimston is Pott Row. Between Grimston
and King's Lynn is Roydon Common, which like Peddars Way
north of Shepherd's Bush is one of the remote, bleak, almost
unpopulated areas of Norfolk. Bus 416 from King's Lynn to Wells
crosses Roydon Common. South of Roydon Common and 4 km ($2\frac{1}{2}$
miles) west of Gayton on the B1145 road is Ashwicken. Of all the
original villages making up the modern parish of Leziate,
Ashwicken alone retains its church, All Saints'. The approach to the
church is by a fine avenue of chestnuts, south from the main road. It
is worth walking out to Ashwicken if one has the time. The church is
chiefly noted for its massive brick buttresses erected in the sixteenth
century by a Tudor squire. Doubtless he lived in the hall adjacent to
the church. The house is now an early nineteenth-century one.
From the main road north of Ashwicken church, fine views may be
seen of a very different countryside to that on Peddars Way, a mere
10 km ($6\frac{1}{4}$ miles) to the east.

   The crossroads with the Roman road from Gayton to Brisley is
800 metres ($\frac{1}{2}$ mile) south of where Peddars Way leaves the
metalled road from Castle Acre to Great Massingham. This is at
Shepherd's Bush. Thereafter to Anmer, Peddars Way follows the
line of the Roman road, which has become a wide cart track.
Between Shepherd's Bush and the A148 road at Harpley Dams,
Peddars Way is crossed by a variety of roads and tracks. After 1 km
(5/8 mile) the walker will cross the B1145 road, and a further 1.2
km ($\frac{3}{4}$ mile) beyond this he will reach Lynn Lane from Great

Good walking along Peddars Way north of Great Massingham.

Massingham to King's Lynn. The 468 bus from King's Lynn to Cromer uses this road. Soon after the junction with Peddars Way, the modern route of Lynn Lane bends north to Grimston. The original route from Great Massingham village was to head south-east into Gayton.

Great Massingham village has a large central pond with an interesting collection of houses round it. The church of St Mary is of thirteenth-century plan with aisles, but a clerestory was added and other fenestration renewed in the fifteenth century. The church is north of the village pond. The village can be approached by Lynn

Lane or by turning right a little further along Peddars Way by a
track which goes past the wireless station and water tower at
TF/788228. Apart from the tower and isolated houses at junctions
of Peddars Way and other paths, the route is lacking in definite
landmarks between Lynn Lane and the A148 road.

Along the section between Lynn Lane and the A148, the surface
of Peddars Way varies considerably. The route dips from
Shepherd's Bush to Lynn Lane before rising in a long climb to cross
the brow of the hill near Little Massingham, followed by a much
shorter descent to the A148 road at Harpley Dams. There are some
particularly fine views across the countryside both on this section
and to the north of the A148 road. From Shepherd's Bush to the
A148 road, the distance is 6 km (3¾ miles); beyond the A148 road it
is a further 4.2 km (2¾ miles) to the B1153 road near Anmer.

The walker should exercise especial care when crossing the A148
road. The road has been realigned at the crossing point with
Peddars Way and a deep cutting made east of the walker's route.
Coming from Fakenham, the main road is extremely straight and
most of the villages have been bypassed. Consequently the traffic
travels very fast. The traffic from the other direction also has had
only gentle curves to impede it.

Just before the road is reached, Peddars Way crosses the line of
the old Midland and Great Northern Joint Railway from Little
Bytham Junction, in Lincolnshire, to Great Yarmouth. No tracks
remain, but at Harpley Dams there is a former crossing-keeper's
house, now enlarged. Apart from a house on the old route of the
A148 road, this is the last house the walker will see on Peddars Way
for 12 km (7½ miles), almost until he reaches Littleport, east of
Sedgeford.

As with the portion south of the A148, this portion of Peddars
Way from north of the main road to Anmer and beyond on to
Ringstead is best walked on one's own or with one very close
companion. The walker will meet very few people. On Harpley
Common, at TF/762279 and at TF/759285, there are round
barrows to the walker's right; another is to his left at TF/755288,
just north of the road from Anmer to Harpley. Yet another is
beyond the B1153 road between Peddars Way and Anmer village at
TF/749295.

As the route does not pass through the villages, this section of Peddars Way is difficult for accommodation. The villages too tend to be missed by the walker and are omitted from many guide books. Those to the west are neatly built and have few inhabitants. Hillington, Flitcham and Anmer are all typical estate villages. The houses are set out in large gardens, and built of the local Snettisham carstone. The churches at Anmer and Hillington were rebuilt by their Victorian patrons, faithfully in an early fourteenth-century style at Anmer. In Hillington church there is an original eighteenth-century organ by the celebrated organ-builder, Snetzler, and a series of monuments to the related ffolkes and Browne families, successive owners of Hillington Hall. This has been demolished, but Anmer Hall still stands, a splendid example of the restrained, late eighteenth-century, gentleman's house, set in its own park.

To the east of Peddars Way are the parishes of Harpley, Houghton and the Birchams, all of which are part of the Cholmondeley estate based on Houghton Hall. Houghton Hall was the residence of a successful early eighteenth-century politician, Sir Robert Walpole, who served as chief minister to both George I and George II from 1717 to 1742. He built the house in the grounds of his ancestral home between 1722 and 1735, using Colen Campbell and Thomas Ripley as architects. There is a very large park containing St Martin's church, of which only the tower and the north aisle windows are older than the eighteenth century. Sir Robert Walpole's church was rebuilt by a Victorian successor, but his model village of 1729, New Houghton, outside the south gate of Houghton Park, at TF/791278, retains a pristine freshness. There are two rows of five semi-detached houses, a set of almshouses and two large farmhouses, all painted white. The village is approached by a fine avenue of trees from the A148 and Harpley village.

Houghton Hall is open only on Thursdays and Sundays: see information below.

Harpley village is less tidy than New Houghton, but is interesting for its farmhouses and for the church of St Lawrence. This flint church was built in the early fourteenth century, mainly between 1292 and 1332 while John de Gurney was rector. His chief work was the large chancel, unusual for Norfolk village churches, but the south aisle and the tower at its west end are also of his time. A century later, the nave and arcades were rebuilt and a clerestory added; of this date too is the south porch. There is much fifteenth-century woodwork – screen, benches and south door – and some contemporary stained glass. On the road from Harpley to the Weasenhams are two long barrows, both probably constructed in the fourth millenium BC. The one north of the road just beyond the trees at TF/810253 is in West Rudham parish, but the other south of the road and visible only as a low mound in a ploughed field is in Harpley. A windmill, at TF/799852, is beside the road between Harpley village and the barrows.

Information

DISTANCE	15.2 km/9¼ miles
STATIONS	none
BUSES	Castle Acre, Great Massingham, Harpley
ADMISSIONS	Houghton Park: Thursdays, 10.00–17.00, and Sundays 14.30–17.00
REFRESHMENTS	Castle Acre, Great Massingham, Harpley
SHOPS	Castle Acre, Great Massingham, Harpley, East Rudham, Anmer
BANKS	none
ACCOMMODATION	Castle Acre
CAMPING	Castle Acre

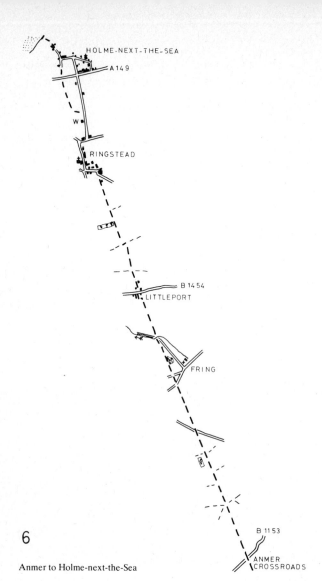

HOLME-NEXT-THE-SEA

A149

W

RINGSTEAD

B 1454
LITTLEPORT

FRING

B 1153

ANMER
CROSSROADS

6

Anmer to Holme-next-the-Sea

6 Anmer to Holme-next-the-Sea
17.1 km/10¾ miles

The final section of Peddars Way from Anmer crossroads to the sea
is clearly defined, from Anmer to Ringstead and from just beyond
Ringstead windmill to the sea. There are very fine views,
particularly to the east. The whole has a great feeling of solitude and
of all the sections of Peddars Way this is the portion best walked
alone. During the early summer vegetation can be very thick in
places, especially in the 1500 metres (1 mile) north of Anmer
crossroads and again in the descent to the Heacham River near
Fring. In contrast, there also portions which are very open, such as
the long stretch with views across to Great Bircham and the part of
Peddars Way east of Red Barn Farm between Shernborne and
Fring. Much of the attraction of this part of Peddars Way is the
variety within comparatively short distances.

From Anmer to Ringstead, the route is remarkably straight; few
directions are necessary, as the path is well signposted. From
Anmer crossroads, where Peddars Way crosses the B1153 road, the
first 1.5 km (1 mile) is along a well-defined path with lush
vegetation either side. In places the undergrowth is waist-high and
at one point it is also necessary to duck under low branches.
Thereafter the way becomes more open and to the east and
north-east there are fine views across to Great Bircham. This is a
flint-built village with a fourteenth-century church. The chief
feature of the latter is that the tower is placed at the west end of the
south aisle, so permitting the west window to light the nave. The
font is of Purbeck marble and the altar table is dated 1640. Both
here and at Bircham Newton (1 km to the north) the woodwork was
renewed by Victorian restorers. Between Great Bircham and
Bircham Newton is Bircham windmill, clearly visible from Peddars
Way, although it has no sails. To visit Great Bircham from Peddars
Way, take either the first or second right-hand turning after Anmer,
at TF/748309 and TF/744318 respectively, reached after walking
1.6 km (1 mile) and 2.7 km (1¾ miles) from the junction of Peddars

Anmer Crossroads where Peddars Way crosses the B1153 road, south of Great Bircham village. From here it is possible to walk to the sea in an afternoon.

Way and the B1153 road. After walking 3.9 km (2½ miles) from the main road, the walker crosses a metalled road, that from Snettisham to Great Bircham.

Snettisham is famed as the place where a number of late pre-Roman Iron Age gold torcs were found in the 1950s. These are now in the British Museum, London, and electrotype copies are exhibited in Norwich Castle Museum. These boards testify to the wealth accumulated in north-west Norfolk in the late first century BC. Snettisham is also the source of much of the local carstone, a soft brown sandstone much used in local building. The church is large, of the fourteenth century, with a fine spire. Snettisham Old Hall is a big seventeenth-century house with Dutch-style gables. Both are outside the village on the Snettisham to Fring road. Snettisham village is a friendly place with a large green.

On the Snettisham to Great Bircham road, and visible from Peddars Way, is Red Barn Farm, a large complex of buildings, most prominent of which is a fine red barn.

Having been mainly uphill from Anmer, Peddars Way from the Snettisham to Great Bircham road northwards for 1.5 km (1 mile) levels out on an open path, again with fine views both to east and to west. After crossing a minor metalled road from Shernborne to Fring, the route descends 30 metres in the space of the next 1.5 km (1 mile) to the Heacham River and the Sedgeford to Fring road. The route has high banks, with thick vegetation on either side, in places approaching coppices. There are good views through the trees, north-east and east towards Fring. Fring is a small estate village with a fourteenth-century church at the south-west end of the houses.

Heacham River in summer is a dry stream bed, but in winter and spring there is more water underfoot, and there is no bridge. Care must be exercised when crossing the stream. After the Sedgeford to Fring road, the route climbs sharply. The ascent is metalled as far as two houses on the right and thereafter is a path through trees. After 200 metres the country levels out, and the path is along the inner edge of a field with a large wood on the left-hand side. At the end of the wood, the walker should go through the gap in the hedge dividing the fields, so that the hedge is on his right when walking north. After 400 metres, where the field boundary turns left, turn left and then after 30 metres turn right following a narrow path which leads past a group of cottages. At the main road, turn right and then after 50 metres turn left to head north along a metalled track.

The directions round the small hamlet of Littleport are well signposted. The main road is the B1454 which leads from Sedgeford to Docking. Docking is 4.5 km (2¾ miles) east of Peddars Way. When seen from the B1153, the road from the south (i.e. the road

Fine walking alongside the parish boundary hedge demarcating Great Bircham from
Shernborne. Peddars Way is used as a parish boundary for much of its line north of
Castle Acre.

from Great Bircham), there is a pleasing view across the small park
of Docking Hall. The late sixteenth-century house was refaced in
the late 1850s. The church is fifteenth-century, standing beside the
main road. West of the village, about 4 km (2½ miles) east of
Peddars Way along the main road, is 'Burnstack' (also known as
'Burntstalk'), a massive structure built in 1836 to the designs of
John Brown, the county architect, as the workhouse of Docking
Union. It cost £9,000 to build and equip and was intended to house

Sir Robert Walpole began New Houghton village in 1729. There are two rows of five pairs of houses on the approach to the south gates of Houghton Hall. All houses are whitewashed brick.

over 500 paupers. In 1845 it rarely held more than a hundred inmates. This large brick building of thirty-six bays in a classical style is worth a detour. On the same main road, the B1454, on the eastern edge of Littleport where Peddars Way crosses the road, is a curious building known as Sedgeford Magazine. It is being converted into a private house, but it is clear that this hexagonal structure with a semi-basement had its origins as a seventeenth-century arms depot. Near here, a pre-Roman Iron Age gold torc was found in 1965, another piece of evidence of the wealth of north-west Norfolk in the first century BC.

At the Magazine, the walker turns left to head north-north-west. After 600 metres, the former railway line from Heacham to Wells-next-the-Sea is reached. It is now a farm track with a cinder bed. Here veer right to walk in a northerly direction with a hedge on one's left. At the end of the field, after 800 metres ($\frac{1}{2}$ mile), turn left and then after 150 metres turn right to resume a north-north-east course. The original line of Peddars Way has been ploughed out in the field north of the former railway track and the diversion takes one only a little way away from the original route. In this area, there are few buildings in sight, the fields tend to be large, and apart from fellow walkers and farmworkers one is unlikely to meet anyone.

After turning right to head north-north-east, there is a hedgerow on the walker's right for 800 metres to the end of the field. Here, on the parish boundary of Ringstead and Sedgeford, between Peddars Way and the road joining the two villages, is a long narrow coppice. Such belts of woodland were planted, perhaps as early as the sixth or seventh century AD, to denote a section of the boundary. A similar piece of woodland is found to the east of the road between Sedgeford and Ringstead and other parts of the parish boundary of Sedgeford are also marked by coppices, most of which can be seen across the fields from Peddars Way. The coppice crossing Peddars Way at its western extremity is not easy to penetrate. There is a path through the edge of the wood taking Peddars Way northwards. Climb the stile, head north-east along a rough track through the trees, and at the beginning of the field resume a north-north-east course with a hedgerow on the left. At the end of the field cross another stile to a footpath which after 20 metres broadens into a green road with hedges on either side. The route is now a descending one and from here on the sea is visible to the north. There are also fine views east and west across the countryside.

The descent down the greenway into Ringstead is about 1.2 km ($\frac{3}{4}$ mile). Towards the bottom there are fine views back up the route of Peddars Way. Where the houses begin the route is metalled, and where the road from Docking joins the route from the east (on the walker's right) there is a pavement. About 100 metres from this

A change in the course of Peddars Way near Sedgeford.

The descent of Peddars Way to the Heacham River at Fring. The route continues by climbing the hill in the background alongside the hedge.

junction, Peddars Way reaches a crossroads with the Ringstead to Choseley road going west to east. The original route of Peddars Way headed north from the crossroads, but this is not now practicable as the path peters out after 300 metres and not even suitable field boundaries remain to record the original route. At the crossroads, therefore, the walker should turn left and head west before turning right after 300 metres to walk northwards through Ringstead village, passing 'The Gin Trap' inn at the foot of the hill and St Andrew's church at the top.

Ringstead is an interesting village. Originally there were two churches to the present village, more properly known as Great Ringstead. That dedicated to St Peter was at the foot of the hill, near Ringstead Bury and Hall Farm, both west of the Ringstead to Sedgeford road. Only the tower survives in the garden of Hall Farm. The present St Andrew's church looks Victorian from the outside and indeed it was restored in 1865 when the north aisle was added, but the basic structure is fourteenth-century. It has been reroofed again, but the brass of Richard Kegell, who died in 1482, records that he had provided for the total reroofing of the chancel. Like many other buildings in Ringstead, the church is of Snettisham carstone.

About 400 metres beyond the church, the walker should turn right and then after a further 250 metres left to resume a northward course. One is now on the road from Ringstead to Holme-next-the-Sea, but east of the original line of Peddars Way. After 500 metres, Ringstead windmill is passed on the walker's left. At the second field boundary beyond the path to the windmill, the route proposed by the Countryside Commission for Peddars Way will turn left and then after 300 metres turn right to resume the original route. This is the path forming the parish boundary of Holme-next-the-Sea and Old Hunstanton. Walk along this for 1 km (5/8 mile) to the A149 main road. Cross the main road with care. There is a slight bend southwards in the main road to the west of Peddars Way and at this point there is no speed limit. After crossing the main road follow the metalled road northwards. After 300 metres there is a bend going right and then left; and a further 400 metres on where the route crosses a small stream there is a bend going left and then right. The metalling of the road ceases about 300 metres beyond this point in the vicinity of Beach Cottage. Peddars Way continues for a further 400 metres to the sea, with the track becoming progressively less well defined.

The walker who has set out from Knettishall Heath and remained on Peddars Way will have walked about 70 km (45 miles). He, or she, will have crossed a great variety of country in walking from south to north through Norfolk and except at Castle Acre will not have been through any place which is home to more than two or three hundred people.

One of the houses in Great Ringstead has an unusual semi-octagonal porch.

Holme-next-the-Sea, the last place on Peddars Way, is in fact one of the most populous. Much of the parish is a bird reserve (see Part Three, section 7). Holme village is east of Peddars Way, the church being almost the last building at the eastern end of the village street, which is at right angles to Peddars Way. Those walking the Norfolk Coast Path will use Holme church as a marker to walk towards when coming from Hunstanton. The church's chief attraction is the exterior: it is bold and big with a splendid tower, really a porch-tower, practically all that survives of the medieval church. The fabric was redone in 1778, when the whole interior was made an open space and the big east window was inserted. The tower and the original chancel were donated by Henry Nottingham and his wife, who died in the first decade of the fifteenth century; their brass is in the chancel.

Information

DISTANCE	17.1 km/10¾ miles
STATIONS	none
BUSES	Anmer, Great Bircham, Sedgeford, Ringstead, Holme-next-the-Sea, Hunstanton
REFRESHMENTS	Ringstead, Holme-next-the-Sea, Sedgeford, Docking, Stanhoe, Hunstanton
BANKS	Hunstanton
ACCOMMODATION	Holme-next-the-Sea, Hunstanton
CAMPING	Holme-next-the-Sea, Hunstanton

Part Three: The Norfolk Coast Path

The Norfolk Coast Path is a route devised by the Countryside Commission and the Norfolk County Council following existing public footpaths from Hunstanton to Cromer. Except between Thornham and Brancaster and between Beeston and Cromer, it is beside the coast or on sea defences of early nineteenth-century date.

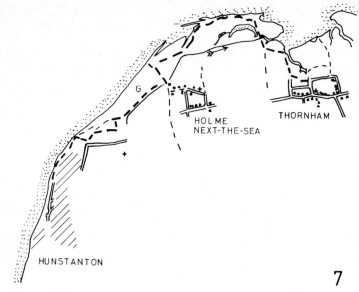

HOLME
NEXT-THE-SEA

THORNHAM

HUNSTANTON

7

Hunstanton to Thornham

7 Hunstanton to Thornham
11 km/7 miles

The first section of the Norfolk Coast Path takes the walker along the top of Hunstanton Cliffs and then by various paths through the sand dunes at Holme-next-the-Sea to the sea defences at Thornham.

Hunstanton is a Victorian creation: the older settlement, now known as Old Hunstanton, is inland, and to the north-east. The railway came to the west Norfolk coast in 1862. Thereafter Hamon le Strange developed a narrow strip along the cliff top beside the railway station as a seaside resort. The result is a collection of terraces and semi-detached houses of no particular marked style. On the front they are tall without being overpowering. On the streets at right angles to the front the houses are mainly in pairs, very broad of beam, plain, serviceable and nondescript. Quite whom Hunstanton was meant to attract was never made clear. The future Edward VII spent some time there in 1871 convalescing from typhoid fever. Having been happy there, he went on to develop the estate at Sandringham which he had bought ten years before. But Hunstanton seems never to have been specifically designed to attract an expensive clientele. There were pullman coaches on some trains in the 1930s and it still has an air of solid respectability reminiscent of Harrogate but lacking the incisiveness of a spa. Perhaps much is due to the departure of the trains in 1968 and the slow drift away of people from the town.

The cliffs, the chief feature of the landscape of Hunstanton, rise from nothing beside the old pier entrance to a height of 30 metres, less than 300 metres to the north. The chief glory of the cliffs is the distinct band of chalk above the native carstone. Most of the houses in the town were built of this stone and somehow they have little warmth in their façades.

Most walkers arriving in Hunstanton to walk the Norfolk Coast Path will probably have come by bus. Hunstanton Bus Station is therefore a convenient point at which to begin.

A terrace of houses in Hunstanton reflecting its origins as a holiday resort created in the 1870s by Hamon le Strange.

From the bus station face east, i.e. with one's back to the sea, and on reaching the road turn left, i.e. north. Follow this road for 200 metres to an open green in front of the Pier Entertainment Centre. Hunstanton Pier was swept away in the gales of 1978 but the onshore amusement arcade remains, a glossy steel-framed building with glass walls.

Here the walker has two choices. He can either descend to the foot of Hunstanton Cliffs or walk along the top of them. To view the cliffs with their banded rocks of chalk above the local carstone, walk across the green to the Pier Entertainment Centre and there turn left to walk to the Lower Promenade. There is a slope leading down to this 100 metres beyond the Pier Entertainment Centre. Walk along the Lower Promenade for about 250 metres. Here the concrete sea defences and promenade end and there are steps up to the top of the cliff. Ascend the steps to the cliff top, and at the top turn left, i.e. north, to walk along the cliff top. The very fine formal gardens of Hunstanton are immediately to the south of the walker when he has reached the top of the cliff steps.

The alternative is to walk along the road to the cliff top. First cross the green opposite the Pier Entertainment Centre, then walk along St Edmund's Terrace and Cliff Parade to the beginning of the walk along the cliff edge. There are formal gardens, putting and bowling greens to the walker's left, and large houses built of carstone to his right.

Where the rough ground, dotted with occasional blue shelters, begins, head for the cliff top walk, which has a fence on the western, i.e. seaward, side. At low tide there are good views of geological formations in the sands, including a possible former causeway stretching out into the Wash. The height of St Edmund's Cliffs gives the walker good views south to the Norfolk and Lincolnshire coastline of the Wash and west across the Wash to landmarks such as Boston Stump. At low tide much shallow water is apparent and there are many sandbanks. Hunstanton Cliffs are an exposed place and when a force 7 gale is blowing walking along them is difficult.

After walking 800 metres ($\frac{1}{2}$ mile) along the cliff top, the walker will pass first St Edmund's Chapel and then Hunstanton Lighthouse. St Edmund's Chapel is the remains of a thirteenth-century building erected on the site where Edmund, King of the East Angles in the tenth century, who was slain by the Danes in 930, arrived in East Anglia on his return from Germany. A more prosaic account of its origins is that it was built as a shelter for travellers crossing the Wash. Hunstanton Lighthouse, a white building 15 metres (49 feet) high, was built in 1830, replacing an earlier wooden structure.

Just beyond the lighthouse is a car park. The walker should walk through this in a north-easterly direction along the cliff edge. At the fence at the end there are two possible routes. The first is to turn right and walk 250 metres to the housing estate, with the putting greens on the walker's right. At the housing estate, turn left and walk 300 metres to the 'Le Strange Arms' hotel. At the crossroads by the hotel, veer right into Wodehouse Road and continue to its end, where one turns left into a minor road which has a short descent. There are houses on both sides of Wodehouse Road; on the next road houses are on the left and there is a green electricity post on the right. At the end of a green fence beside a water pump carry straight on and proceed to the entry to the golf course. At the golf course turn right to walk beside the stream.

The alternative route from the car park is to walk through the sand dunes. There is a public footpath forming the official Countryside Commission route of the Norfolk Coastal Path at this point. At the north-west corner of the car park take the dog-leg exit which leads to the footpath through the dunes. This involves going left, right and then left again before the path is apparent. It then proceeds at just above sea level to a metalled road. Follow this, passing the club house of the golf club on the left, to a gate just after the road has turned right. Turn left on to the path which leads beside a stream, to walk along the south-eastern edge of the golf course.

When walking alongside the golf course, do not walk across the fairways or along the path down the centre of the golf course but remain on the path on the south-eastern edge which runs beside the stream. The stream is of clear, fresh water and much aquatic life can be observed. Holme church lies ahead. The last part of the path, which is 1.3 km (1 mile) long, is beside a caravan park. At the end of the golf course walk straight on from the end of links along the path beside the caravans, which is clearly marked by railway sleepers and signposted.

The path ends at a bridge over the stream. Here turn left on to the final part of Peddars Way to walk north towards the sea (for description of Holme-next-the-Sea, see Part Two).

The walker now has two alternative routes, both of which lead to paths round the seaward side of Holme Nature Reserves. For the first, turn right at Beach Cottage and walk along the rough track which serves as a car park at the western edge of the nature reserve.

The walker may prefer to continue past Beach Cottage and walk along Peddars Way towards the sea. To continue on the Norfolk Coast Path, he should walk to the car park beside Peddars Way and just after the entry point (not the exit) turn right on to the path which goes beside the edge of the golf course. Hole 8 is on the left. This path follows a course through bushes to open ground with sand dunes on the left. For the next 600 metres it is well defined along the top of the dunes, with a creek on the left and good views of the beaches and of the sand headland known as Gore Point. This section of the Norfolk Coast Path has a great feeling of solitude and communion with nature.

The path reaches the car park of the Holme Nature Reserve and thereafter is defined by slatted boards. Keep to these and do not walk haphazardly on the sandbanks. When the slatted boards cease, take to the path between the two sets of dunes. This section can be slow going. After 800 metres ($\frac{1}{2}$ mile), the path reaches an entry to the Bird Observatory. Here, turn right from the dune path, ascend the steps and turn left, i.e. east, to walk along the path on slatted boards above the stretch of water known as Broad Water, a part of the observatory. This leads to paths along the sea banks leading south to Thornham.

Holme Bird Observatory was established in 1962. It can be visited by obtaining a permit from the Warden's House, directions for which are given at the entry points to the observatory. Like the much larger Holme Nature Reserve to which it is adjacent, Holme Bird Observatory is a Site of Special Scientific Interest. A great many different types of both migrating and native birds can be seen here. Holme Nature Reserve, through which the route of the Norfolk Coast Path goes, includes coastal flats, dunes and marshes as well as a lagoon.

From the path on the northern side of Holme Bird Observatory, Broad Water can be seen to the south. At the end of the slatted path, turn right, i.e. south, on to the sea bank leading to Thornham. After 700 metres turn left on to another sea bank and walk east for 500 metres before turning right to walk beside Thornham Creek. After 150 metres cross the first arm of the creek by the bridge and

Walkers on the sea bank near Thornham.

then walk south for 400 metres to a footpath along a raised bank which is reached by turning right where a field is fenced off. This path is overgrown in places, and can be avoided. Those who walk the path reach a metalled road leading south into Thornham village. Turn right on to this and walk south to the centre of the village, reaching Thornham church after 250 metres. The alternative is to continue on the metalled road from Thornham Creek which goes south to the A149 road and then to turn left on to the main road and to walk 500 metres to the centre of the village. Thornham church is then on the left, and the village stores on the right on the opposite side of the road.

Thornham Creek is a delightful place, quiet and unobtrusive, with small boats moored beside the jetties. It was used as a commercial harbour until the Great War. Nathaniel Woods sailed the *Jessie Mary* into Thornham Harbour for the last time in 1914, and lived for twenty-two years more as the respected last merchant of Thornham. His vessel was a two-masted cargo brigantine, of 100 tons.

Thornham Church shows how scarce good building stone is in north Norfolk. When in the fifteenth century the nave was heightened and a clerestory was added, the pier bases were raised and the former nave arcades reused. There is a screen of 1488, given after the rebuilding, and a pulpit of 1631. The south door is fifteenth-century, as are some misericords.

Thornham village is largely built of chalk blocks. The better-class houses are flint or brick. Porch House has a date stone of 1638 on the porch, but this flint house could be earlier. Both Thornham Hall and the Red House are eighteenth-century brick houses. To build a (now disused) malting at the eastern end of the village brick was combined with chalk blocks. There are brick houses adjacent as part of Malthouse Farm. The school, to the west of this, is weird but, like several strange Victorian Gothic buildings of its date, 1858, not ineffective.

Information

DISTANCE	11 km/ 7 miles
STATIONS	none
BUSES	Hunstanton, Holme-next-the-Sea, Thornham
NATURE RESERVES	Holme-next-the-Sea, Thornham
REFRESHMENTS	Hunstanton, Holme-next-the-Sea, Thornham
SHOPS	Hunstanton, Holme-next-the-Sea, Thornham
BANKS	Hunstanton
ACCOMMODATION	Hunstanton, Holme-next-the-Sea, Thornham
CAMPING	Hunstanton, Holme-next-the-Sea, Thornham

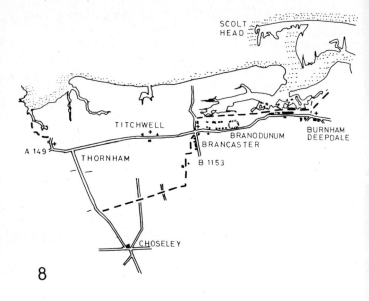

8

Thornham to Burnham Deepdale

8 Thornham to Burnham Deepdale
10 km/6¼ miles

The walk from Thornham to Burnham Deepdale involves a fairly lengthy detour inland between Thornham and Brancaster, as no suitable paths exist along the few coastal defences on this portion of the Norfolk Coast Path. From Brancaster to Burnham Deepdale the walk is along a marsh-side path.

At Thornham church face east, looking along the main A149 road. Walk along the road through the village for 600 metres to a road on the right signposted for Choseley. Walk along this road in a southerly direction for almost 2 km (about 1¼ mile). The road climbs quite steeply out of Thornham and good views across Thornham and Titchwell marshes can be seen looking northwards. When Titchwell was enclosed in 1786 and the marshes were partly drained, techniques of retaining the newly-won land did not include banks round the marshes. Hence no walk is possible along the marshes. Having climbed the hill, the walker will pass a farm barn on his left. At the field boundary south of this, which is the parish boundary of Titchwell and Thornham, turn left along the northern side of a thick coppice. This thins out and after 500 metres there is a path between hedges. The path is very wide and crosses first the Choseley to Titchwell road and then after 600 metres a further road. The section between the two roads has gates at either end, and there are large farm barns at the second road. At the left-hand turn in the path, walk north into Brancaster village, arriving opposite Brancaster church.

From the path, Choseley can be seen. This is the least populous of all Norfolk civil parishes. Only ten inhabitants were recorded in the census of 1971. There is no church. As with Heacham to the west, the area is famed for lavender growing. Spring and early summer are good times to see the lavender harvest.

Brancaster village is laid out mainly along the A149 road. It is an attractive place having at its eastern end the site of Branodunum. The road on the eastern side lies in the ditch of what was once a

An inland stretch of the Norfolk Coast Path, heading north to Brancaster.

Saxon shore fort of the fourth-century defences of Roman Britain. A local squire found the stones of the walls a tempting quarry and used them to build a vast malt house in 1770. In more recent times a planning authority has joined with an uninspired builder to erect one of the ugliest housing estates ever to be described by that grotesque term 'executive development'. There are other horrors of this nature in Brancaster and at Brancaster Staithe, east of the old Roman fort, where in the fourth century the Dalmatian Cavalry were stationed.

The older houses of Brancaster are pleasanter and the pubs

The sign of 'The Ship' at Brancaster is a model of the *Victory*.

The route of the Norfolk Coast Path follows the creek at Brancaster Staithe.

reflect the prosperity of the area. On the outside wall of 'The Ship' is a large, intricate model of a fully rigged ship. The name of the vessel is the *Victory*. This is the beginning of the area with Nelson associations.

'The Ship' is almost opposite St Mary's church, a fourteenth-century structure, to judge from the arcades. There is a good fifteenth-century font cover which rises inside itself when the font is being used for baptisms. The royal arms are late, being those of William IV and dated 1832.

At the church, the walker has two choices. He can either follow

the official route of the Norfolk Coast Path or turn right and walk
along the A149 road east for 2 km (1¼ mile) to Brancaster Staithe.
On the left the walker will pass Staithe House, a pleasant large
Georgian House set back from the main road; 100 metres after this
there is a turning to the left leading to Brancaster Staithe and the
path along the marshes.

The official route devised by the Countryside Commission is to
walk north along the road past the west door of St Mary's church
and then after 300 metres turn right on to the marsh path from
Brancaster to Brancaster Staithe. This is what it says, a marsh path,
and very wet. Boots are advised for those who walk this 2 km (1¼
miles).

The walk along the marsh path affords good views over the creeks
in front of Brancaster. With the exception of the land of Brancaster
Golf Course, which belongs to the Royal West Norfolk Golf Club,
on the northern side of the creeks, this area is National Trust land.
The land owned by the National Trust extends to Scolt Head, the
western end of the island beyond Norton Creek, to the east. Good
bird watching and excellent botanical expeditions are to be had on
Scolt Head, but to visit it requires a permit. Boats sail from
Brancaster Staithe and are advertised.

It is worth walking the 1.5 km (1 mile) from Brancaster village
out along the road to the golf club for the views east along the
creeks. There are also good views north of the sea and north-east of
Scolt Head. Scolt Head is an important example of how new land is
laid down by the deposition of sand against an existing headland;
another is Blakeney Point (also National Trust land), further east.

From Brancaster Staithe eastwards there is a good path along the
marsh side, for the 1.3 km (¾ mile) to Burnham Deepdale. Since
Brancaster Staithe had no church of its own, the custom grew up
long before the Great War for the inhabitants of Staithe, as it is
known locally, to worship at Burnham Deepdale. Indeed the war
memorial is to the men of Deepdale and Staithe.

Brancaster Staithe is a sailors' harbour and can be noisy, but away
from the bustle the views north across the marshes and the creeks
are very fine.

At the end of the path beside the marsh there is a metalled road

The round tower of St Mary's church, Burnham Deepdale, was built by the Saxons.
Inside the church is a font whose carvings depict the labours of the months.

leading northwards across the marshes and south to Burnham Deepdale village. Opposite is the beginning of the sea bank round Deepdale Marsh and then Norton Marsh. The Norfolk Coast Path continues along the top of the bank.

Many will wish to visit St Mary's church at Burnham Deepdale, an odd mixture of Victorian rebuilding and early survivals, where even the Victorian does not seem out of place. The early work is a Saxon tower with an internal upper doorway, a fourteenth-century north arcade, a twelfth-century north door and what some guide books describe as a Norman font; though in reality it is the work of a Saxon mason and he knew what was important to an agricultural community. In January and February the winter enforced rest: a man with a drinking horn signifies the former month, a man warming his feet the latter. In March the hard work began with digging and in April the fruit trees were pruned. In May it is the festival of Rogationtide, the three days before Ascension Day when each parish walked its perimeter and declared its lands in the ceremony of beating the bounds: how else in a world without maps are fields to be defined? In June, the ground was weeded before scything in July and binding a sheaf in August. In September the corn was threshed and in October it was ground, but no baking of bread is shown. Instead in November a beast is slaughtered preliminary to the feast in December. With interlaced ornament, friezes and mythological beasts to complete the design, the font at Burnham Deepdale church is a rare gem worth walking miles to see.

From the end of the marsh path from Brancaster Staithe, turn right and south on to the metalled road. At the junction with the A149, turn left on to the main road and walk 150 metres to the church. Beyond the church at the junction of the A149 and the secondary road to Burnham Market there are some interesting cottages, with a mixture of brick and flint walls.

Information

DISTANCE	10 km/6¼ miles
STATIONS	none
BUSES	Thornham, Brancaster, Burnham Deepdale
NATURE RESERVES	Brancaster Manor, Scolt Head

REFRESHMENTS	Thornham, Brancaster, Brancaster Staithe
SHOPS	Thornham, Brancaster, Brancaster Staithe, Burnham Deepdale
BANKS	Burnham Market
ACCOMMODATION	Thornham, Brancaster, Brancaster Staithe, Burnham Deepdale, Burnham Market
CAMPING	Thornham, Brancaster

9 Burnham Deepdale to Wells-next-the-Sea
16 km/10 miles

The walk from Burnham Deepdale to Wells-next-the-Sea is first
along coastal defences to the sand dunes between the sea and Overy
Marshes, and thereafter within the sand dunes and through the trees
of Holkham Meals. After Holkham Gap, the route is behind the
trees and adjacent to the meadow grazing of Holkham and
Wells-next-the-Sea. The last 1.6 km (1 mile) is along the
promenade of the seaside resort of Wells-next-the-Sea.

Beginning at Burnham Deepdale church, the walker should
retrace his steps westwards for 100 metres to the road to Brancaster
Marsh. Here turn right and walk 150 metres to rejoin the Norfolk
Coast Path at the beginning of the sea defences round Norton
Marsh created after the enclosure of 1821. Climb up on to the sea
defences and walk north-east along them. After 1.2 km (¾ mile) the
defences have curved round to head east. About this point there is a
stile to cross. After the stile the upkeep of the path changes; before
it, the way is well-trodden, after it, the undergrowth and grass tend
to be waist high. Walk on for 2.5 km (1½ miles) to another stile.
Despite the undergrowth, it is better to walk along the top of the sea
defences rather than try walking along the foot of the defences on
the seaward side, where there is no path and the ground is marshy.
After the second stile, the path turns south-east, and is much better
defined. After 500 metres, the sea defences turn south-west; 800
metres (½ mile) further on, they turn sharply west. Here the walker
should turn left, i.e. east, and cross the River Burn on a raised bank.
At the end of the bank cross a stile and walk through the field
towards Burnham Overy windmill. On the other side of the field is
the A149 road, where turn left and walk for 600 metres into
Burnham Overy Staithe. Thereafter there is a footpath for 300
metres to 'The Hero' public house.

When the Countryside Commission have established the full
route of the Norfolk Coast Path, there will be a footpath inside the
field on the south side of the A149 road, which will make walking

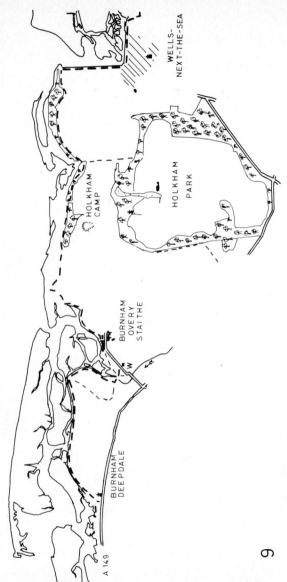

9

Burnham Deepdale to Wells-next-the-Sea

safer. Those using either the 1:50,000 or 1:25,000 Ordnance Survey maps, respectively numbers 132 and TF84, might be misled into thinking that at the stile at the end of the sea defences, after crossing the River Burn, it is possible to walk along a footpath into the harbour of Burnham Overy Staithe. Unfortunately the public footpath marked on the maps leads only to a landing stage and to a garden wall, and no access is possible to the harbour. Walkers must therefore cross the field which leads to the windmill.

By taking the path round the marshes, the walker misses completely the majority of the seven Burnhams. What he gains is the views over the creeks and the great solitude of the coast. There are also good views southwards from the sea defences to where the land rises above Deepdale Marsh and Norton Marsh. Overy Marsh is outside the sea defences and lies between the final part of the walk along them and the village of Overy Staithe.

Many, however, will wish to visit one or more of the Burnhams, and perhaps also the Creakes further inland. These parishes formed the smallest of the ancient administrative divisions of Norfolk, Brothercross Hundred, which functioned from before Domesday Book (1086) to the establishment of Poor Law Unions in 1834.

Burnham Deepdale has already been described. Immediately east is Burnham Norton. The village forms a loop off the A149 road, about 3 km (2 miles) from Burnham Deepdale. The houses are mostly of chalk lump and brick. St Margaret's church is impressive, set over a kilometre (more than half a mile) south on the road to Burnham Market. At TF/835427, it is almost on the parish boundary. The chief features of the church are a round tower, probably Saxon, thirteenth-century aisles and arcades, with a contemporary south door, and a rood screen of 1458 given by William and Joan Groom. There is a near-contemporary hexagonal pulpit, given by John and Katherine Goldale: he is shown with four Latin doctors on the paintings of the five panels. East of the parish church, at TF/838248, are the remains of Burnham Norton Friary, a Carmelite house founded in 1241 and enlarged in 1353. All that remains is a fourteenth-century gatehouse, approached from a secondary road behind the school. From the church, retrace steps north for 250 metres and turn sharp right to go south-east; the road turns right after 400 metres, and the entry to the Friary is 200 metres further on.

Burnham Norton Friary can also be approached from Burnham Market by the B1155 road east of the small market town, turning left some 300 metres after Burnham Ulph church. The Friary is 300 metres along this road. Burnham Market consists of three of the ancient Burnhams, namely Burnham Westgate, Burnham Ulph and Burnham Sutton. The main body of the small market town is set between the churches of the first two. Burnham Westgate church (St Mary's) has a big west tower of the early fourteenth century, with contemporary arcades, chancel and north chapel. Externally it looks large, but internally it appears small. The church is just outside Westgate Hall, built in 1783 to designs of Sir John Soane by a Norwich builder, using yellow brick. Soane built elsewhere in Norfolk, principally Shotesham Park south of Norwich.

Burnham Ulph church, with its churchyard backing on to North Street, where the bus stop is, is much less pretentious, consisting only of a nave, a chancel and a south porch. The chancel arch is late Norman.

The town of Burnham Market has eighteenth-century bow-fronted houses set on either side of a village green. The houses are mostly large and have an air of quiet prosperity. Inhabitants in 1845 included an excise officer, a stationer, two solicitors, two surgeons, and a tea dealer, and the town still has the air of an earlier age. Shopkeepers today include antique dealers, wine-merchants, and a butcher selling home-killed beef.

Burnham Sutton was 1 km (5/8 mile) south-east of Burnham Market town on the B1355 road to Fakenham. The scant remains of St Ethelbert's church are at TF/836417. Further south, above the valley of the River Burn, are the remains of North Creake Abbey (TF/856395). Founded in 1206 as a hospital, and soon transformed into an Augustinian priory, it became an abbey in 1230, and had a flourishing life for nearly three centuries but collapsed as a religious house in 1504 when all the canons died of plague within a week. The income was seized by the King's mother, Lady Margaret Beaufort, for her new foundation, Christ's College, Cambridge. Because of this, exceptional muniments remain in the college archives. The remains of the abbey are spectacular: substantial thirteenth-century arches of the crossing space and the adjacent transepts, chancel and side chapels. Parts of Abbey Farm, adjacent to the church, incorporate other fragments of abbey remains. Among the benefactors of Creake Abbey was William Calthorpe, whose brass, in academic dress and holding a church, has been transferred to North Creake Church. An earlier benefactor to the village church was a William Carletone who gave the great east window in 1301. Of similar date in St Mary's church, North Creake, are the south doorway, the south porch and the chancel. The nave is fifteenth-century with a fine hammer-beam roof above: the wall-plate is decorated with angels with spread wings. The royal arms are those of Charles I and date to 1635.

North-east of Creake Abbey is Burnham Thorpe. At the south end of the village is the site of the former rectory, at TF/856406. Here, or perhaps in the barn next to the public house, was born a son to the rector's wife: as the plaque proclaims, Horatio Viscount Nelson of the Nile, Vice-Admiral of the Blue, was born on 29 September 1758. His father, the Rev. Emanuel Nelson, was not a rich man; his successor in the living was, and immediately demolished the rectory on being appointed to the parish in 1803. The rector now had a modern house much nearer All Saints' church. The church is a splendid thirteenth-century building with a later chancel whose east window is one of the finest pieces of fourteenth-century work in the county. The restoration of 1890, done as a memorial to Nelson, was very true to the medieval building. Beyond the Nelson relics, Burnham Thorpe church is worth going to see as a church. There is a bust commemorating Nelson between the graves of his parents. He wished to be buried in his native Norfolk; victory decided otherwise, and he is buried in St Paul's Cathedral, London. Each year, on the anniversary of the battle of Trafalgar, (21 October) the church flies the white ensign from the flagpole on its fifteenth-century tower. The flag is a full-size replica of that flown from the *Victory* at Trafalgar; the original is within the church.

The pub in Burnham Thorpe was renamed 'The Nelson' but retains the older fabric and fittings. The sailor held a party there to commemorate his promotion to Captain in 1793, and the place looks little changed since two hundred years ago. The flint barn next door has a thatched roof on a fine timber frame. The village of Burnham Thorpe is a mixture of chalk lump and flint with brick used for the corners of buildings and sometimes intermixed in the walls. Most of the older roofs are thatch; a few are red pantiles.

Burnham Overy, like Burnham Thorpe, is east of the River Burn: the other Burnhams are to the west of their river. Best approached from Burnham Market, Burnham Overy parish contains two villages. Inland is Burnham Overy Town, the smaller settlement. On the river is a large mill, combining both a watermill and a windmill: the sails and cap have been removed and the only power now used is water and electricity. The road bends sharply north just after crossing the river and the main hamlet of Burnham Overy Town is found round the stump of a preaching cross. One of the houses of the terrace unexpectedly has large statues guarding its doors. The church of St Clement occupies a knoll above these houses, and the road to Burnham Overy Staithe bends round its churchyard and other houses adjacent. Keep a sharp eye for traffic, as this is a dangerous set of corners. The church has a central, Norman tower between the nave and the chancel, but the transepts have been demolished, as has one storey of the tower. The result is a squat building, with a seventeenth-century cupola replacing the former uppermost stage of the tower, and incredibly big windows.

To the north of the church is Burnham Overy Staithe, 1.2 km ($\frac{3}{4}$ mile) along Mill Road. There are fine views north over the marshes from here, and even better views from the top deck of a bus. Burnham Overy Staithe is set out along the main A149 road, which the road from the church meets almost in the centre. Far to the west, at TF/835437, is Burnham Overy Mill, a large brick watermill of 1737 with an adjacent miller's house. Like the mill in Burnham Overy Town, it is still working. The A149 road crosses the River Burn at this point. The walker coming from the village will already have passed the windmill at TF/837438, retaining the cap and sails and open to the public. It was built in 1814. Facing the harbour in Overy Staithe is the former Moorings Hotel. Viewed from the marsh, or from the walk along the sea bank, this and the adjacent maltings make a picturesque group. Once a sizeable coastal port, Burnham Overy Staithe is now a sailing place, and like all the other harbours on the north Norfolk coast it is filled with enthusiasts and their craft. Most of the buildings in Overy Staithe are of brick, including the local hostelry, 'The Hero'. The signboard leaves no doubt who is meant. Nelson did sail from Overy Staithe both as a boy and while pensioned off on half-pay in the 1780s.

To explore the Burnhams fully takes a whole day, but it is worth the effort, because the walker can take in so much more than just the stretch of coast between Burnham Deepdale and Burnham Overy Staithe.

From the 'The Hero' the walker on the Norfolk Coast Path should walk due north along East Harbour; if he has come from walking round the sea defences to the A149 road, he should turn left at the public house. After 50 metres turn right to a path which leads to the sea defences round Overy Marsh. These are reached after a walk of another 50 metres. Go through the gate on to the path along the sea defences. This involves turning left almost immediately and heading out in a north-easterly direction. The walk along the defences bends to the east after 800 metres ($\frac{1}{2}$ mile), and after a further 300 metres turns north, i.e. left. It continues north for 400 metres and, where the defences turn right, the path descends to follow inside them on the landward side. After a further 250 metres turn left, i.e. north; the path beside the defences peters out after another 300 metres.

From here the walker should head east among the sand dunes, preferably on the innermost, landward side, as this is the most sheltered route. After 1.2 km ($\frac{3}{4}$ mile) the edge of the woods of Holkham Meals is reached. From here fine views can be had looking inland towards the banks of Holkham hillfort, a lowland fort built in the second half of the first millenium BC, probably as a trading post. The fort, at TF/875447, is sited beside Decoy Wood and is not easily seen from within the Meals. It can be approached from Burrow Gap, reached after walking 500 metres along the path through Holkham Meals.

The entry to the path through Holkham Meals is almost at the southern edge of the wood. For the next 2.5 km ($1\frac{1}{2}$ miles), the walker has a woodland route through pine and birch trees.

Alternative routes exist between the end of the sea defences at Burnham Overy Staithe and Holkham Gap. The first is to walk north of the woodlands of Holkham Meals and through the sand dunes. There is a well-worn track close to the northern edge of the woodlands. The second alternative is to walk outside the dunes, on the northern side, and thus along the hard sand of the West Sands of Holkham Bay. These stretch from the entry to Burnham Harbour to the entry to Wells Harbour, known as The Run. They are a fine safe beach, ideal for relaxing and free from any commercialisation.

Holkham Bay is large and fronts the very large parish of Holkham, much but not all of which is enclosed within Holkham Park. Here in the eighteenth century a transformation took place both of the landscape and of agricultural practice. The Coke family by then had risen to the largest estate in Norfolk. The family fortunes were founded by Sir Edward Coke, who was a lawyer and Speaker of the House of Commons in Elizabeth I's reign. Holkham, the parish, was bought in 1610; from 1707, it was transformed, and the process took the whole of the eighteenth century to complete.

The village, just off the main A149 road around TF/892440, was again rebuilt in the 1890s. It is the first set of buildings the walker will see if he goes due south on the road from Holkham Gap, is reached after walking 800 metres ($\frac{1}{2}$ mile) and consists of a good inn, 'The Victoria', houses, a post office, a craft shop and teashop combined, a school, and, at the entrance to the park, a set of almshouses. From the gates, it is a walk of 1 km (5/8 mile) to Holkham Hall.

Holkham Hall is the result of a long exposure to Italian fashions and Italian architecture. Thomas Coke, its builder, was away on the Grand Tour for six years from 1712. From 1734 until his death in 1759, he was actively engaged in constructing the house: it was completed by his widow in 1761. Thereafter, Lancelot ('Capability') Brown did the grounds, but these were essentially transformed by another Thomas Coke, the celebrated Coke of Norfolk, who so improved his immense estate – it covered 50,000 acres (about 20,000 hectares) and included land in thirty-one Norfolk parishes when he died in 1842 – that his rents rose by one

A pleasant walk through Holkham woods between the sea and Holkham Hall.

thousand per cent. Around the great house, the visitor will see
sheep: the Norfolk fold-course is still applied on the Holkham
estates to improve the sandy soil. Although there is a deer park,
near to the northern entrance, most of the great park at Holkham is
farmland. Only the large cricket lawn to the north of the house and
the lake to its west have a recreational use.

The house is open on Thursdays from June to September and on
Mondays and Wednesdays in July and August; other attractions at
the Hall have longer hours: see Information.

The house is austere, as austere as the eighteenth century can be.

The south front of Holkham Hall. It was designed by William Kent for Thomas Coke, first Earl of Leicester, and completed in 1761.

There is a central block and four oblong blocks at the corners. Except for the great kitchen, these are not included in the walk round. Even when still building, Holkham Hall was shown off to visitors; by 1772, the tourist trade was thriving. Visitors enter by the Marble Hall, which rises the whole height of the house: it sets the tone, for Holkham Hall was designed to show off the first Earl of Leicester's collection of statues and paintings. Most of the first Thomas Coke's statues are in the Statue Gallery, which occupies the western side of the central block. On the south side are the Drawing

Room, the Saloon and the South Dining Room, each of which has an exceptionally good collection of paintings. Finest, perhaps, is the Gainsborough of Coke of Norfolk in country dress, painted in 1782 to celebrate his presentation to King George III of the address from the House of Commons requesting that the war with the American colonies be ended. In the eastern block the southern room, the Landscape Room, is so named from its landscape paintings by the seventeenth-century artist Claude Lorraine; the other rooms in the east block are state bedrooms, their décor including Brussels tapestries. Visitors leave the house by the great kitchen.

Housed in nineteenth-century outbuildings are the Holkham Pottery, founded by the Countess of Leicester in 1957, and a large collection of bygones exhibited since 1979 in the former stables and coach houses, for which there is a separate admission charge. It is well worth seeing.

The entrance to the formal gardens of Holkham Hall is to the right of the entrance to the house. They occupy the terrace on the west and south sides of the house, and facing the central portico are the fountains. Both gardens and fountains are extremely attractive.

The monument to Coke of Norfolk erected to his memory by his tenants in 1842 can be seen looking north from the house; looking south, the obelisk (of 1729) can be seen on the top of the hill behind Holkham Hall. Both are aligned on the central axis of the centre block of the house. South of the obelisk is the avenue, 2.5 km ($1\frac{1}{2}$ miles) long, also on the axis of the house. There is a fine view north over the house from the obelisk; southwards, the avenue stretches as far as the eye can see. The trees which make up the avenue are currently (1980) being renewed, essentially in alternate clumps; this does not detract from the view. To walk round the house, see the exhibition of bygones and walk down the full length of the avenue to the South Gates and the Triumphal Arch beyond would take a complete day.

Much of the park at Holkham is wooded, as is the northward side of the walk along the Norfolk Coast Path from Holkham Gap to Wells-next-the-Sea. Those who have visited the house or grounds of Holkham Hall should retrace their steps to Holkham Gap, and there turn right on to the path on the southern edge of Holkham

Meals. Those who are continuing the walk from Burnham Overy Staithe should come out of the woods and walk south to the car park. After going through the gate, turn sharp left to walk in a north-eastern direction. The path bends round to face east. After 2 km ($1\frac{1}{4}$ miles), the walker is facing south for about 50 metres. There is a track leading south into Wells-next-the-Sea, but the walker should turn left to walk east, and then north-east round the northern edge of the caravan site. Camping is also possible here at the Pinewoods Caravan and Camping site.

At the end of the walk inland from the pine trees of Holkham Meals, the walker has reached the northern end of the river wall opposite the lifeboat station. There he should cross the road which leads to the beach, walk round the bank (on which walking is not permitted) and turn right to walk the 1.6 km (1 mile) along the path on the river side of the bank. Walkers on the road, i.e. western, side of the bank can find the traffic heavy. After 500 metres the weary can cross to the entry to the caravan and camping site and take the train (summer only) which runs to the seafront at Wells.

On reaching the end of the river walk, which is the northern side of the harbour basin, the walker should continue south to the edge of the car park opposite the shops, then turn left on to the sea front. After 50 metres he is opposite the lower end of Staithe Street, with 'The Golden Fleece' public house on the corner.

Staithe Street is the main shopping street of Wells-next-the-Sea, a jolly place full of the locals in the daytime and quiet at night. The quay has two remaining grain warehouses, only one of which is still used. Other, disused ones line other streets back from the harbour. On the quay itself a big crane seems to be permanently parked; to see it unloading the grain is an impressive sight. On a good day, up to five coasters can be seen moored beside the harbour wall. When the sea has reached high tide and on a stormy day, the water almost laps the top of the sea walls. In the January 1978 gales a coaster was, in fact, deposited on the quay; and Wells was one of the worst hit places in the 1953 floods. The old railway station, then still in use, and 500 metres inland, was flooded to above the level of the platforms. The old railway station is the terminus of buses from Norwich and from King's Lynn and Hunstanton. The latter routes,

The quay at Wells-next-the-Sea is a bustling grain port.

numbers 416, 417 (summer only), 418 and 419, also have a stop at the top of Staithe Street.

Near the bus stop in the town is a pleasant green called The Buttlands with fine eighteenth-century houses set round it; one has interesting topiary work round the doors. It is a pleasing contrast to the flint houses nearer the quay. Some modern houses in Wells reflect good design, with brick and flint interwoven. The church is at the southern end of the town, approached by the High Street. It looks medieval, but in fact is a total, and faithful, Victorian rebuilding after a disastrous fire in 1879. The priest's door to the chancel is fifteenth-century work.

The busy port with its fishing boats and small sailing craft riding at anchor on the flowing tide is a pleasant place for the walker to stop and recharge his batteries. It is a centre for excursions, too: Holkham Hall can be visited from Wells, as can Little Walsingham, 7 km (4½ miles) inland. In contrast to the flint and chalk lump houses of the coast, Little Walsingham is dominated by timber-framed houses, set on the square around the parish pump (still working). There is a massive parish church, restored after a disastrous fire on 14 July 1961. Beneath the spire and roofs are a chancel with a north chapel, two aisles, a wide nave, and a south porch. The north chapel has the tomb of Sir Henry Sidney, the local landowner and relative of the poet; he died in 1612 and is commemorated by a good example of Jacobean funerary art.

Elsewhere at Little Walsingham is the Guildhall Museum and the various buildings associated with the pilgrimages of Walsingham, both Anglican and Roman Catholic. A reintroduction of a medieval practice, these extend to the Slipper Chapel at Houghton St Giles to the south, where pilgrims left their shoes and from where they walked barefoot to the shrine of the Virgin at Little Walsingham. Henry VIII was among the last of the medieval pilgrims. The previous night he had stayed with Sir Henry Fermour at the latter's new mansion at East Barsham. The house is not open to the public, but can be seen from the main B1105 road, at TF/916338. To the east of this at Great Snoring is the Old Rectory, another large brick building of Tudor date, built by the Shelton family in the 1520s. Both the church and the village are worth seeing; a good south arcade and a royal arms of James II can be seen in the church, and the village houses are flint and brick. North-east of Great Snoring is Great Walsingham, where St Peter's church is good fourteenth-century work.

All these villages – Little Walsingham, East Barsham, Great Snoring and Great Walsingham – are in the valley of the River Stiffkey, whose sea outlet is east of Stiffkey village, but is best approached by the B1105 road from Wells-next-the-Sea (bus services 450–454).

Information

DISTANCE	16 km/10 miles
STATIONS	none
BUSES	Burnham Deepdale, Burnham Market, Burnham Overy Staithe, Holkham, Wells-next-the-Sea
ADMISSIONS	Burnham Thorpe church: 14.00–1700, Burnham Overy windmill: summer only, Holkham Hall – house: Thursdays, May–September, 10.00–17.00; Mondays and Wednesdays, July and August, 10.00–17.00, Holkham Hall – pottery and bygones: daily, 10.00–17.00
NATURE RESERVE	Holkham Meals, also known as Holkham West
REFRESHMENTS	Burnham Market, Burnham Thorpe, Burnham Overy Staithe, Holkham, Wells-next-the-Sea
ACCOMMODATION	Burnham Market, Burnham Overy Staithe, Wells-next-the-Sea, Little Walsingham
CAMPING	Pinewoods, Wells-next-the-Sea
SHOPS	Burnham Market, Wells-next-the-Sea
BANKS	Burnham Market, Wells-next-the-Sea

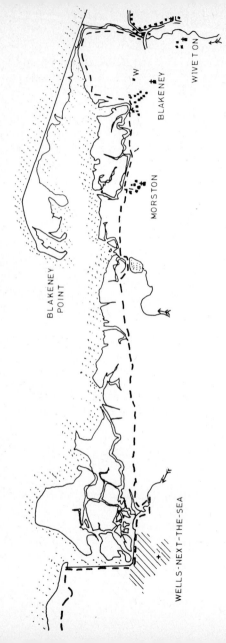

10   Wells-next-the-Sea to Blakeney

10 Wells-next-the-Sea to Blakeney
11.7 km/7¼ miles

From Wells-next-the-Sea to Blakeney, the route of the Norfolk
Coast Path is along a well-defined footpath between the inner edge
of the salt marshes at Wells, Warham, Stiffkey and Morston and the
beginnings of agricultural land. Between Wells and Blakeney,
except in Morston harbour, the walker is unlikely to meet many
people, except other walkers. The route lies away from the villages.

Standing on Wells quay outside 'The Golden Fleece' public house
at the bottom of Staithe Street, the walker should face east to begin
the walk to Blakeney. After walking 75 metres along the quay, the
walker reaches the beginning of East Quay, where the main road
turns right (i.e. south and inland). On the corner is Charles Ward
(Ship Chandler), a white building with the fenestration painted
blue. Keeping this on his right, the walker should head east along
East Quay, passing the Custom House on the right (with the royal
arms outside) and a sitting area with tables and seats on the left.
After 50 metres, pass 'The Shipwright's Arms' public house on the
left and then a slipway. Where the road forks, after about 300
metres, take the left-hand fork, next to a boat repair yard on the
left. This is marked 'Public Footpath'. After a further 20 metres,
climb up on to the sea defences, beside a sign marked 'Private
Property, No Parking'. This involves a half-left turn and a climb of 2
metres. The path on the sea defences is well trodden, between
purple flowers at the appropriate season.

Following the sea defences, turn right after 500 metres and then
after 300 metres turn left. After the left-hand turn, the path narrows
considerably for a walk of 400 metres along the sea defences. At the
end of the sea defences turn left and go through the gate, following
the path through the bushes, which may be at face height. The path
first goes north and then bends to turn west. It is still narrow, but
the vegetation is now only at knee height. As the path becomes
wider, the vegetation becomes less dense and it is more grassy
underfoot.

East of Wells-next-the-Sea the Norfolk Coast Path follows the path at the edge of the mud-flats. In the photograph the belt of trees protecting the entrance to the harbour at Wells can be seen in the background.

Thereafter the path in Warham is on the inner (landward) edge of the eastern part of the Holkham Nature Reserve, which is a National Nature Reserve managed by the Nature Conservancy Council. The whole of the saltings, the flats and the dunes are protected. Access is restricted to certain well-defined roads and paths. Along these there are foot bridges over major and minor streams, of which only one, that which runs east-west separating the outer group of Warham Salt Marshes from the inner marshes, is named. It is Stonemeal Creek.

   The path along the marsh edge is not hard underfoot, and after rain it is apt to be boggy. Care should be exercised to avoid slipping. Where the path is on firm ground, the grass can be longer than expected and unusually moist, and again care should be taken.

   While easy to follow, the path along the inner edge of the salt marshes is by no means straight. After 500 metres, it turns right to negotiate the edge of the marsh and a large, oval, water-filled pit. Where the path turns left to head east, it is narrow for 30 metres, and single file is recommended. Thereafter it broadens out for a further 500 metres before reaching Garden Drove, a tarmacadam-surfaced road heading south and inland. Here turn left and then immediately right to take a partly surfaced road heading east. Follow this for 1.1 km (¾ mile), crossing a metalled road, Cocklestrand Drove, after 500 metres. Where the metalled road turns right, i.e. south, continue straight on in an easterly direction along a well-defined footpath for 3.2 km (2¼ miles). After about 1.5 km (1 mile) a number of buildings will be seen on the right at Coneyford Plantation. To the north, i.e. on the walker's left, are Stiffkey Salt Marshes. These are National Trust property and a Site of Special Scientific Interest. The protected area here is purely of coastal saltings.

   After passing Stiffkey Greens, the path veers right, and after 400 metres turns right and then left to ascend the barrier at the mouth of the River Stiffkey. After 200 metres, the walker turns left at the end of the barrier and walks in a northern direction for 150 metres before turning right, i.e. east. After 1.4 km (1 mile) turn right, i.e. south, and then left to follow the path to Morston Harbour.

   On the eastern side of Morston Harbour, ascend the sea bank beside Morston Creek and follow this eastwards for 800 metres (½ mile). Where the bank turns south, descend to the path heading east across the marshes. This, following Agar Creek, is well defined between knee-high plants. After 700 metres (almost ½ mile) there is a southerly turn in the path which then reverts to an easterly course. Hereafter, it is possible to ascend a low bank along the marsh edge. This takes the walker into Blakeney. After crossing the stile at the end of the houses, walk south past 'The Red House' to the road along Blakeney Quay. Turn left on to the quay and walk 300 metres

To the south of the surviving nave of the former priory church at Binham, now used as St Mary's parish church for the village, are the conventual buildings of the Benedictine priory. In the foreground of the photograph is a bake-oven once in the kitchen. Beyond this is the undercroft of the dormitory and the refectory. The crossing space of the monastic church can be seen in the background. The piers retain their dressed stone and much of their decoration.

to the lower end of Blakeney High Street, with the car park on the seaward side and opposite to this, in front of the mound, a set of public conveniences.

The description of the route has said little of the fine views across the salt marshes towards the sea and also from Stiffkey Greens onwards of Blakeney Point. Blakeney Point was the first nature reserve to be established in Norfolk. This Site of Special Scientific Interest, given to the National Trust in 1912, covers 581 hectares (1436 acres). Like Scolt Head, it has been formed by the progressive action of sand being deposited by the sea on the edge of an existing sandbank. Access to Blakeney Point is by boat from Morston.

The route of the Norfolk Coast Path from Wells-next-the-Sea to Blakeney tends to avoid the villages. Warham, the first parish to the east of Wells, has two churches surviving, and there was originally a third. All Saints' church, around which most of the village is situated, is now a shadow of its former self: the tower is gone, both aisles are cut down to single bays now utilised as transepts, and a Norman font originally having carvings of the labours of the months is lying cut into an octagonal shape with the surviving faces defaced. It seems to symbolise the decay of the village. The favoured church was St Mary's, where the Turner family installed a mausoleum as a north chapel to the chancel, contemporary high box pews and a triple-decker pulpit. The priest's doorway on the south side of the chancel, above which a buttress rises, is earlier. South of the two churches and on the other bank of the River Stiffkey is Warham Camp, an Iron Age plateau fort with bivallate defences enclosing 1.4 hectares ($3\frac{1}{2}$ acres). The bank is impressive, standing 2.7 metres (9 feet) above the interior; the silted ditches are a similar depth below this level and originally the present top of the bank was about 7.5 metres (25 feet) above the bottom of the flat-bottomed ditch. Because of the concentric nature of the defences, it has been suggested that Warham Camp may have been reused by the Danes in the tenth century.

Stiffkey is famed in the twentieth century for the Rev. Harold S. Davidson, who was vicar of the parish. Deprived of his living for spending his life in Soho – he was known as 'the prostitute's parson'

– he died in 1924 after being mauled by a lion, his partner in a circus act at Skegness. Earlier Stiffkey had been the centre of Sir Nathaniel Bacon's estate. He began building Stiffkey Hall in 1578; the gatehouse to the south, beside the river, is dated 1604. Of his house, only the west range and half the north range survive: the original great hall and the east range are respectively partly and wholly demolished. Bacon had no son, and his eldest daughter married the heir to the Townshend estate based on Raynham Hall. After its completion, the Townshends had little need of another large house comparatively near and Stiffkey Hall was allowed to decay as early as the eighteenth century. Sir Nathaniel Bacon wished to be remembered, and his monument in the church of St John the Baptist, Stiffkey, was erected before his death in 1615. By then, St Mary's church was already ruined. East of Stiffkey village and above the river is Camping Hill. Here the game of Camping is supposed to have been invented. It is an early version of Rugby football, played between two teams of unlimited size, usually large in numbers, and over a large field.

Neither Warham nor Stiffkey is easily accessible from the route of the Norfolk Coast Path, since both villages lie 1–2 km (¾–1¼ miles) to the south. Golden Drove and Cocklestrand Drove, right-hand turnings heading south from the Norfolk Coast Path, at TF/943438 and TF/949438 respectively, both lead after crossing the A149 main road to Warham All Saints; Warham St Mary is west of this on a minor road, and Warham Camp is south of Warham All Saints at TF/944409. Paths to Stiffkey are few. There is a footpath leading south at TF/970440 which leads into Hollow Lane, reaching the village at its western end; Bangay Green Way, the turning for which is at TF/973440, is a walk of 1 km (5/8 mile) to the eastern end of Stiffkey village.

Worth visiting, if time permits, but beyond Stiffkey to the south, is Binham. From the A149, take the minor road south at TF/971431 and after 300 metres take the left-hand fork. This is just past 'The Victoria' public house. Walk south-east for 800 metres (½ mile) and then bear right, avoiding Cockthorpe, and follow the metalled road for 2.7 km (1¾ miles) to reach the eastern end of Binham village.

Near Morston, the Norfolk Coast Path follows a wide gravel path beside one of the many creeks within the mud-flats of the north Norfolk coast.

Binham is an unspoiled village with a wide village street (now the B1388 road) separated by houses from a triangular village green. The houses at Binham are flint with brick or stone dressings; most have thatched roofs. Most people, however, visit Binham for its priory church, founded in 1091 by Peter de Valoines, and built between then and the early thirteenth century. Good views of the priory remains are to be seen on the walk south to Binham from across Binham River. Access to the priory, now the parish church of St Mary, is from the minor road from Binham to Warham to the north-west of the village. Facing the onlooker is the west front built by Prior Richard de Parco (prior between 1226 and 1244) of which the great window was blocked by brickwork in the eighteenth century. It is thought to be the earliest example of bar tracery in England. Architectural evidence suggests it was new work to complete a nave (now used as the parish church) where building work had ceased in the mid-twelfth century. The nave is one of the great glories of Norman England and with the aisles blocked off – an effect of the diminution of the church's size at the dissolution – the tiered effect of arcade, triforium and clerestory only serves to emphasise the solidity and chunkiness of the construction. The church was cut down in 1540 to seven bays of the nave, those west of the pulpitum, on which a new east window was built. The two other bays of the nave, the crossing space and the apsidal chancel can be traced in stone piers and low walls east of the present church. To the south of the church are the excavated remains of the monastic quarters.

The first village the walker approaches on the route of the Norfolk Coast Path is Morston, with its creek full of yachts. Apart from being the point of embarkation for Blakeney Point, Morston is chiefly interesting for its much rebuilt church set in a treeless and almost graveless churchyard beside the main road. There is much brick in the structure of the tower, which like the rest of All Saints' church is late thirteenth century in date. Noteworthy is the brass, below the altar, to the Rev. Richard Makynges who died in 1596. It is the only Elizabethan brass to a clergyman in Norfolk.

South of Morston is Langham. The Victorian novelist Captain Frederick Marryat retired to Langham Hall after the Napoleonic Wars to write stirring sea stories, of which *Mr Midshipman Easy* is probably the best known.

The tower of Blakeney church has been the beacon the walker can see ahead all the way from Wells. It stands south of the town, set between trees both to the north and to the south. Like most coastal church towers, its height recalls its original purpose: to be a sight for incoming mariners. At the east end of the chancel on the northern side is a smaller tower, likewise built to aid navigation. Internally, the chancel is striking, with a rib-vault of four bays and a

Most Norfolk villages have a village sign. That at Blakeney reflects the earlier
importance of the village as a port.

complex seven-light lancet window at the east end. As with most
north Norfolk churches there is a good nave roof, with
hammer-beams combined with arched braces, and angels set on
horizontal timbers. The roof is not dissimilar in date from the west
tower of 1435.

Blakeney town is built of flint and brick. Of the older buildings,
only 'The Red House', at the west end of the harbour, is wholly of
brick. It was built in the eighteenth century, and is the first house
the walker passes on reaching Blakeney. From here there are good

Blakeney harbour still thrives but is used only by pleasure craft and by local fishermen.

views across the harbour. Blakeney Harbour has much bustle and
many boats. Mains drainage has meant that the village has many
cottages occupied only in the summer, and the trade is geared to the
expensive kind of yachting, done for show rather than serious
sailing. The town is architecturally unexciting with one exception,
the undercroft of the former guildhall, which is brick, vaulted, and
of fifteenth-century date. The skin is of stone, as presumably the
upper storey originally was. Salt was the trade which provided
Blakeney's late medieval wealth, but few of the houses on the High
Street are much older than the early nineteenth century.

Information

DISTANCE	11.7 km/$7\frac{1}{4}$ miles
STATIONS	none
BUSES	Wells-next-the-Sea, Blakeney
NATURE RESERVES	Holkham East; Blakeney Point
REFRESHMENTS	Wells-next-the-Sea, Stiffkey, Morston, Binham, Blakeney
SHOPS	Wells-next-the-Sea, Morston, Blakeney
BANKS	Wells-next-the-Sea, Blakeney (restricted days), Holt
ACCOMMODATION	Wells-next-the-Sea, Stiffkey, Morston, Blakeney, Binham
CAMPING	Wells-next-the-Sea, Stiffkey, Morston

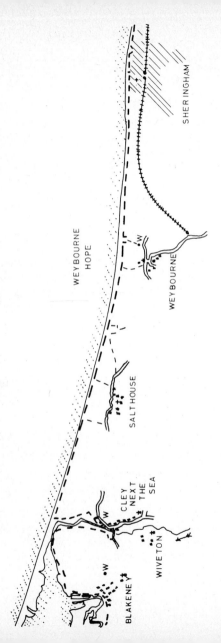

11 Blakeney to Sherringham

11 Blakeney to Sheringham
18.5 km/12½ miles

The walk from Blakeney to Sheringham falls into two parts. From Blakeney to Cley-next-the-Sea, the walker follows the sea defences enclosing Blakeney Marshes, and these are followed also from the windmill at Cley to the sea at Cley Eye. Thereafter the walk is along the coast edge, first beside the shingle bank and then after Weybourne Hope along the cliff top.

At the public conveniences in Blakeney face north and walk out towards the sea along the well-worn track on the top of the sea defences. These follow a northerly course for 850 metres (just over ½ mile) and then turn east. Here the path descends from the sea bank and heads north-east across the saltings to Cley Channel. At low water it is possible to cross Cley Channel and walk along the inner edge of The Marams forming Blakeney Point, also known as the North Side of Blakeney Channel. At high tide, it is possible to get a boat from either Blakeney or Morston to Blakeney Point. The area is owned by the National Trust and is a nature reserve, famed for its bird life, the small creatures of the foreshore and as a place to study how the coast has been laid down. These coastal flats, saltings and dunes cover 581 hectares (1,436 acres) and were established as a nature reserve in 1912, the first such area to be established in Norfolk.

Those walking the Norfolk Coast Path should turn right, i.e. east, where the sea defences round Blakeney Marshes turn right. Thereafter walk in an easterly direction for 1.5 km (1 mile) before turning right again. Where the defences turn south, some walling can be seen in the field to the south and west. This is the indistinct remains of Blakeney Chapel, erected in the thirteenth century and now only a few sparse ruins. Originally its tower served to indicate the entry to Cley Harbour Channel. The walker then goes south for 1.2 km (¾ mile) before turning right and then left to walk south again for a further 300 metres to reach a point above the A149 main road.

While walking round the sea defences, there are good views west across Blakeney Harbour and on a good day west as far back as Wells: the red and yellow lifeboat house is clearly visible. There are also good views south of Blakeney itself, with two disused windmills visible east of the town. On the walk south from Blakeney Eye, there are good views east across the marshes, and south of Cley. Cley windmill is especially prominent. The church to be seen is Wiveton church, rebuilt in the late fourteenth century but incorporating an earlier tower and an earlier chancel. It has a good series of sixteenth-century brasses.

Going south from Wiveton is the River Glaven, which has a picturesque valley well worth taking a day to walk. The first part is along the B1156 road from Wiveton to Letheringsett past the shell museum at Glandford. Letheringsett church is partly Anglo-Saxon, and beside the bridge is a good eighteenth-century brewery founded by the Hardy family. South of Letheringsett, minor roads allow one to follow the river though Little Thornage and Hunworth, but the upper reaches are more difficult of access. Hunworth is a particularly attractive village with a fine church, partly of pre-Conquest date, a watermill at present being restored and a fine seventeenth-century house and adjacent barn. Hunworth Green to the east is worth visiting. The roof of Stody church, to the west of Hunworth, has good carpentry, the roofs of nave, chancel and transepts meeting as a rib-vault over the crossing space. The town of Holt to the north of this part of the River Glaven is famed for Gresham's School, founded in 1555 by Sir John Gresham and endowed by his son, Sir Thomas Gresham, the English agent in Antwerp, the financial centre of late sixteenth-century Europe. He defined inflation as 'bad money driving out good'. The town of Holt is a jolly place with a couple of good bookshops, a decent bakery and all those things one hopes for in a small country town. Those exploring the Glaven valley on a day off from walking the Norfolk Coast Path should note that no buses run out from Holt to either Blakeney or Cley after 13.00 on weekdays.

The walker on the Norfolk Coast Path from Blakeney has been walking above the western bank of the River Glaven. When the sea defences reach the A149 he should turn left, i.e. east, and walk

The windmill at Cley-next-the-Sea is one of the most famous landmarks on the north Norfolk coast. It was built in 1711 but has been restored in the twentieth century.

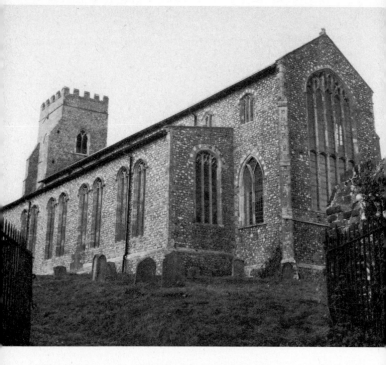

Salthouse church reached its final form in the fifteenth century. Its size and scale remind us that Salthouse was an important port until the Meyne channel dried up in the early eighteenth century. This view is from the south-east.

across the river to where the bank ends. Here there are two choices. The first is to turn left along the path which leads behind the houses of Cley village and to Cley windmill. The second is to climb down from the bank on to the road into the village and to turn left at Three Roads End, a T-junction, and then walk through the village to the windmill.

Cley village is partly strung out along the main A149 road, and partly on the road leading south from Three Roads End. The main road has houses of various dates from the sixteenth century onwards, mostly build of flint. More modern buildings are on the Holt Road leading south past the green and the church. St Margaret's church is large with a north-west tower, a bold fifteenth-century porch and various features erected in the fourteenth century. These include two transepts, both ruined, the south one with distinctive tracery to its south window already derelict in 1600, and the clerestory and supporting arcades. Cley church is the creation of prosperous merchants who traded from the harbour which used to occupy the green to the north of the churchyard. John Greenway was one who gave stalls and misericords. Though it is not visible from the sea, the church is a salty place which breathes the wealth which made its building possible.

Part of that wealth arose from the milling of grain and its carriage. On the route of the Norfolk Coast Path is Cley windmill, perhaps the best preserved of all Norfolk windmills, a brick tower mill, retaining its cap and sails, but now a private house.

From Cley windmill, the sea bank which forms the route of the Norfolk Coast Path heads north-east and then after 400 metres north for a further 1 km (5/8 mile) before reaching the sea. In places the bank is difficult to walk and walking along the road to the east of it may be more sensible. There are good views from the bank of Cley, and also east across Cley Marshes and Salthouse Marshes. Both of these are National Trust property and famed as ornithological centres. Both are bird sanctuaries. Respect those crouching in the long grass of the lower slopes of the sea bank; they are intent on watching the many species of birds who use Cley Marshes as a staging post on their migrations.

Where the sea bank and the road from Cley meet the sea, there is a coastguard lookout station. Here turn right to walk the Norfolk Coast Path east to Weybourne Hope. The official path runs at the foot of the high shingle bank; it is possible with difficulty to walk the shingle bank itself. If you do not wish to visit Salthouse, walk east for 6.4 km (4 miles) to the beginning of the cliffs of Weybourne Hope.

Those wishing to visit Salthouse will find a footpath south after

The marshes at Cley and Salthouse are famed for the variety of birds which can be seen there. On the stream beside the A149 main road at Salthouse, ducks and waders swim. In the background of the photograph is Salthouse marsh with the shingle bank beyond.

2.5 km (1½ miles), another footpath to the village after 3 km (2 miles) and a road after 3.5 km (2¼ miles), all distances being from Cley Eye where the coastguard station is. The second is the most convenient, leading to the centre of the village below the church. Salthouse is smaller than Cley, and lacks its prettiness, but is no less interesting. Sir Cloudesley Shovel, the celebrated seventeenth-century mariner, was born here. Several generations earlier, the boys of Salthouse were taught in the chancel of St Nicholas' church,

The cliffs at Weybourne Hope seen from the shingle bank at Kelling Hard. The deep water anchorage was beneath the breakers.

and their graffiti of ships adorn its stalls and screen. The church, perched high above the former port, was built late in the fifteenth century and completed only in 1503. It clearly had the dual purpose of school and church. It is more spartan than Cley church. To the east, along the main road, there is a duck pond where many of the water birds come inland.

It is possible to walk from Salthouse to rejoin the Norfolk Coast Path at Kelling Hard, by walking along the A149 in an easterly direction from the village for 600 metres to where the main road

bears right. A track straight ahead leads on the seaward side of
Gramborough Hill. Take this, and walk east for 800 metres ($\frac{1}{2}$ mile)
before turning right, i.e. south. After 200 metres turn left, i.e. east,
and walk along a track crossing a small stream. After 100 metres,
the track turns left, i.e. north, and after 100 metres bears right
before reaching Kelling Hard. This is a large shingle area in front of
radio masts and other disused installations, mainly dating from
World War II.

About 1.2 km ($\frac{3}{4}$ mile) beyond Kelling Hard and the military
buildings is the beginning of the cliffs of Weybourne Hope. There is
a road leading south from a car park beside the beach to the village.
The beach at Weybourne Hope has interesting geological
formations.

Weybourne village is of flint, with pretty gardens beside the road
from the sea. In the centre of the village is All Saints' church, a
complex building incorporating a partly ruined priory reusing
various parts of an Anglo-Saxon church with a central tower. This
tower still stands, now oddly placed beside the present chancel, and
there is another tower at the west end of the present nave. The
latter was erected in the fifteenth century, as was the south porch.
Weybourne church is an impressive mixture of surviving buildings
and ruins.

From the church the walker has two choices. One is to retrace his
steps and return along the road to the beach. At the beach, turn
right, i.e. east, and walk along the path which ascends the cliffs of
Weybourne Hope. At the top there is a coastguard house. To
navigate round this, turn right at the wall, walk south along the side
of the wall to where the wall turns east, and there turn left to walk
east for 20 metres; at the path turn left, i.e. north, walk to the sea,
and at the cliff edge turn right to continue walking along the cliff
edge path to Sheringham. The other route from Weybourne church
is to face east and climb the hill on the road. After 100 metres there
is a footpath on the left-hand side of the road. After 400 metres,
turn left on to a metalled track leading past Weybourne mill. After
600 metres this leads to the sea. At the cliff edge, turn right to
continue walking the Norfolk Coast Path into Sheringham.

Weybourne mill is a brick tower mill with the miller's house
attached. The sails are only partly extant.

The tower mill at Weybourne has had its sails restored in the late 1970s. The old grain store is now a private house.

The chalk and sand cliffs between Weybourne and Sheringham. Sheringham golf course is on the right of the picture.

   At Weybourne Hope, the cliffs rise almost sheer from the sea and ships could shelter here almost unobserved. Its reputation gave rise to the jingle:

   He who would old England win
   Must at Weybourne Hope begin.

The government of Queen Elizabeth I took the threat seriously, for in 1588 plans were drawn up for elaborate sea defences from Weybourne to Cley-next-the-Sea which would have allowed the heights of Weybourne Hope to act as an observation point.

From Weybourne Hope and from the cliffs going towards Sheringham there are fine sea views. The climb from the beach at Weybourne is followed by a fairly level portion for 2.5 km (1½ miles) to the foot of Skelding Hill. Here, beside the beach, is Robin's Friend, a lump of chalk rock visible at low water. The climb up Skelding Hill, beside the Sheringham Golf Course, is fairly steep, with a subsidiary summit about half way up. There are very good views along the coast from the top. It is just possible to see Wells lifeboat station, and Blakeney church is distinctly visible: look for a church tower set between trees.

From Skelding Hill, the walker descends into Sheringham. The descent east is steeper than the ascent from the west. The golf course is still adjacent. At the foot of the cliffs, where the hill declines into a flatter area, can be seen the Royal National Lifeboat Institution lifeboat shed at Sheringham. The lifeboat is launched off a turntable, before being released down the slipway. The West Promenade ends at the lifeboat shed.

At the end of the golf links, there is a path between fences leading to The Leas. Take this and walk east on to The Leas, a pleasant area for sitting out, with shelters. From The Leas descend to the West Promenade, either by the slope about half way along or by the steps at the eastern end. Walk along the West Promenade for 200 metres and at the slope up to the town, bear right and ascend the slope, to arrive outside the 'Two Lifeboats Hotel' at the sea wall end of High Street, in Sheringham.

Sheringham is the best of the resorts on the north Norfolk coast; it is a splendid, jolly place, as full of life in mid-winter as in mid-summer. The locals are friendly and welcoming to visitors. They know fashion is fickle and have other ways of making a living besides the tourist trade. The big hotels, some supposedly of architectural significance, have mostly been demolished and in their place blocks of flats and maisonettes have been built on The Esplanade. Only one vast hotel remains; the 'Burlington', a large, boring building set back from the end of the upper promenade. It bears the date 1899.

On the corner of The Driftway is a flint house, perhaps of Tudor date, refurbished in the 1930s. Otherwise the buildings of

Fishing for crabs is an old Sheringham industry. During the day the crab pots are left to dry.

Sheringham seem unremarkable at first sight. But look above the shop fronts and there are little gems like the arts-and-crafts timberwork of the group on the bend of the High Street opposite the town clock. Sheringham is a place to linger, with a good bookshop, and almost opposite it a shop selling home-made chocolate. The town has good pubs with warm comforts; the bread shops produce the real thing, home-made and of high quality. The theatre operates all the year round, but the steam railway is run by enthusiasts and has a much more restricted service in winter than in summer. It utilises the former Midland and Great Northern Joint Railway's line from Sheringham to Weyborne: see Information.

Above a slipway, with lobster pots and crab pots littering the street not far away, is the shed which used to house Sheringham lifeboat. Here is kept the *Henry Ramsey Upcher*, thought to be the only remaining rowing lifeboat still in existence. A small lifeboat museum is attached: see Information.

At the end of the the High Street, the concrete cliffs rise 20 metres; this is a treacherous coast with seas men dare to speak of with hushed breath. Even on a mild winter's night the lower promenade is awash at high tide, and it is not unknown for spray to crash over the top of the defences of the town.

Information

DISTANCE	18.5 km/12½ miles
STATION	Sheringham
BUSES	Blakeney, Cley-next-the-Sea, Salthouse, Weyborne, Sheringham
ADMISSIONS	North Norfolk Railway: exhibition all the year round, 09.30–17.00 (varies in winter); train service from Sheringham to Weyborne Station, Saturdays and Sundays from May to September, weekdays July and August
	Sheringham Lifeboat Museum: June to September, weekdays 10.00–17.00
NATURE RESERVES	Blakeney Marshes, Blakeney Point, Cley Marshes, Salthouse Broad
REFRESHMENTS	Blakeney, Cley-next-the-Sea, Salthouse, Weyborne, Sheringham
SHOPS	Blakeney, Cley-next-the-Sea, Salthouse, Weyborne, Sheringham
BANKS	Blakeney (restricted days), Holt, Sheringham
ACCOMMODATION	Blakeney, Cley-next-the-Sea, Salthouse, Weyborne, Sheringham
CAMPING	Kelling Heath (near Weyborne), Beeston Regis

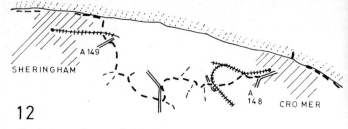

12

Sherringham to Cromer – the inland route

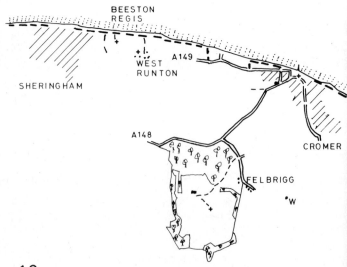

12

Sheringham to Cromer – the coast route

12 Sheringham to Cromer
7.7 km/4¾ miles

The final section of the Norfolk Coast Path is partly a coastal walk
and partly an inland walk on the route to be designated by the
Countryside Commission. However, it is possible to walk nearly all
of the distance between the seaside resorts of Sheringham and
Cromer with only one very slight deviation inland from the cliff
edge. Both routes are given here.

The official route is 7.7 km (4¾ miles); the route along the cliff
edge is 6.2 km (about 4 miles). Both are a pleasant afternoon's
walk.

Both routes are the same from Sheringham to the foot of the hill
to the east of the town known as Beeston Bump. Beginning at 'The
Two Lifeboats Hotel', which is on the corner of the High Street and
the ramp to the Promenade, the walker should descend to the lower
promenade. This involves walking west for 30 metres and then at
the foot of the ramp turning right and back to walk east. Then walk
east for 100 metres to a small slipway. To negotiate this, turn right,
and after 10 metres bear left; after another 20 metres turn left and
walk across the slipway head. An immediate left turn and then a
right turn takes one on to the East Promenade. After 250 metres,
a series of steps up the cliffs will be seen; public conveniences have
been built beside them. Ascend the steps to a sloping path which
leads past a putting green. At the top of the sloping path, turn left
to another sloping path which leads past houses on the right to a
well-defined path which goes up Beeston Hill.

In the winter (approximately November to April), the steps at the
end of the East Promenade may be closed for repairs and
rebuilding. If this is the case, the walker should follow the route to
the slipway and there walk along Ocean Road, which leads from the
south to the slipway. After 150 metres, turn left into Cliff Road and
then after a further 100 metres turn left and then right into Vincent
Road. After 200 metres, the walker will have reached the end of
Vincent Road and be opposite the end of the ascending path beside

Erosion is slowly destroying the sand cliffs of north Norfolk. Between Sheringham and Cromer there are several detached pieces of rock. This one at West Runton has a band of chalk above the sand.

the putting green. Here, he should continue straight on along the sloping path which leads past houses on the right and the putting green on the left to the well-defined path which begins at the foot of Beeston Hill.

At the foot of Beeston Bump, the alternative local name for Beeston Hill, the walker should climb the ascending path to the top of the hill. The climb is about 1 in 20, ascending 30 metres (100 feet) in 600 metres. Towards the top it is steeper, and steps have been cut. There is a triangulation point on the top of Beeston Bump and seats are provided.

From the top of Beeston Bump good views can be had of the surrounding countryside. At certain times the two-car diesel rail trains which ply between Sheringham and Cromer and afterwards go from Cromer to Norwich can be seen either approaching or leaving Sheringham Station. The railway line is easily seen, being set on a slight embankment. Due south of the railway line an ivy-clad stone building can be seen. This is the remains of Beeston Priory, an Augustinian foundation of 1216. It is partly demolished and the adjacent Abbey Farm has been built of the materials. The present house here is eighteenth-century and of flint. The ruins are not yet open to the public, but it has recently been taken into guardianship by the Department of the Environment as an Ancient Monument.

From the top of Beeston Bump there are good views too of the sea and along the coast. The tower of Cromer church is particularly prominent.

The descent eastwards from Beeston Bump is by a well-defined path, but care should be exercised as it is much steeper than the ascent from Sheringham. At the hedge at the foot of the hill, the walker has two choices. Either he can walk ahead along the coast or he can turn right along the hedge and follow the Countryside Commission route of the Norfolk Coast Path.

The official route is along a footpath heading south. After 300 metres cross the railway, exercising care to ensure that no train is approaching. To the east the view along the track is blind after 300 metres; to the west one can see almost into Sheringham Station. After crossing the railway, follow the path south for another 300

Between Sheringham and Cromer the inland walk climbs through birch woods.

metres to the main A149 road. Cross the main road with care, as this part of it is derestricted.

After crossing the road take the old road to the right and walk along it for 150 metres. Here turn right and walk past Beeston Hall, and along an ascending bridleway for 1.6 km (1 mile), to where it reaches woodland set on hills. Turn left and walk east for 250 metres to where the path forks. Take the right-hand, ascending fork and climb Beacon Hill. This is a fairly narrow path but wide enough for a Landrover or other vehicle. The ascent bears right and south after 80 metres. At the top of the hill, reached after a climb of 400 metres, there is a meeting place of several paths. Those walking the Norfolk Coast Path should continue straight on in a south-easterly direction, reaching a minor, metalled road from West Runton to Aylmerton after a walk of 700 metres (about ½ mile).

On this section of the walk from Beeston Hall to the road there are good views north from the foot of the hill, and at the junction of paths at the top of the hill the character of Beeston Heath can be observed. From here too, looking north-east, the nearby Incleborough Hill, with its golf course on the southern side, can be seen. At TG/183414, there are the remains of the so-called Roman Camp. It is an unexcavated earthwork of ill-defined type. Roman pottery has been picked up in the vicinity and a similarity with late Roman signal stations on the Yorkshire coast has been suggested. The heathland is National Trust property: 28.73 hectares (71 acres) were purchased in 1923–4 and a further 15 hectares (37 acres) in 1970. The latter are on Beeston Regis Heath, the former on West Runton Heath.

At the fork just east of the Roman Camp the walker should continue straight on. After 200 metres walk from the Roman Camp the road from West Runton to Aylmerton is reached. At the crossroads so formed, the walker should go straight ahead and then almost immediately turn left on to a descending path. It is not possible to reach this path from any point further along the metalled road back to West Runton.

The path heads first north-north-east and then turns north-north-west before reverting to north-north-east. The descent is considerable, over 30 metres in 450 metres. The road back to West Runton keeps to the top of the ridge above the wooded pathway. After 600 metres, the path turns right and east. After 100 metres the trees end and the route skirts the golf course for 250 metres before going along the edge of a field for a further 350 metres. Here there is a sharp left-hand turn just after a small stream has been crossed. After 70 metres the walker will meet a better defined track, partly metalled and running north-south. Here, he should turn right and face almost due south. Ignore the right-hand turn after 30 metres and follow the left-hand path. After 200 metres this bears left and the walker is facing south-east; 100 metres

Horses and riders ascending the bridleway to the east of the Roman Camp at Beeston.

further on turn left and face north. After 100 metres the path turns right and the bridge under the railway can be seen dead ahead.

After the wooded walk, there are good views of the countryside. The buildings of Manor Farm beside the railway viaduct are of flint and brick construction.

The walker should go past these, across the metalled road which leads past the farm, and go under the railway line ascending Stone Hill. 300 metres from the railway viaduct the path bears left and goes between Roundabout Hill and Broom Hill. After 550 metres the path runs beside the railway line and turns due east. After

walking 350 metres between the railway line and occasional minor
industrial buildings, the walker will come to Holt Road, Cromer.
Here turn left and walk for 300 metres to Crom. r Beach Railway
Station, the official end of the Norfolk Coast Path.

The Countryside Commission route for the Norfolk Coast Path
from Beeston Bump is an inland walk, and can be very hot; two
kilometres inland the breeze felt on the coast is lacking, and many
will wish to walk the coast itself rather than go inland.

There is a footpath along the cliff edge from the foot of Beeston
Bump, going eastwards. Follow this. After the first field, it is
necessary to go inland about 30 metres to cross a crevasse. Very old
notices here announce that there is no right of way, and that people
walk at their peril. Heed the latter; but ignore the former. There is
an established public footpath along the edge of the cliff and
through the caravan site. Thereafter it is a pleasant walk of 1.4 km
(almost 1 mile) along the cliff edge to a metalled road which leads to
West Runton Beach. There is a small car park here and public
conveniences. On this section, the walker will pass two churches.
The first is All Saints', Beeston Regis, externally a fifteenth-century
building with a good monumental brass to John Deynes and his wife
in the chancel: he died in 1527. The second church is Holy Trinity,
West Runton, basically fourteenth-century but with an earlier
tower.

As the walker goes along the coast, good views can be seen of the
coast and its structure. Much of the rock here is chalk. In the sands
below other geological formations can be seen.

At West Runton Gap, negotiate the car park and cross the road,
walking to the far, i.e. eastern, side of the hut with seats. The path
begins behind the hut. Walk north-east for 100 metres and then
turn right to face east, thus walking along the cliff edge. The walk is
along a good path for 800 metres ($\frac{1}{2}$ mile) but this becomes difficult
at the end of the caravan park, where a fence projects over the cliff
and is difficult to negotiate. Here, either go back to the gap in the
stake fence about 40 metres back, or climb over the stake fence into
the caravan park. The eastern fence of the caravan park has a gap in
it leading to scrub land; go through it and turn right, i.e. south.

There is a path through the scrub to the main A149 road. An alternative is to walk down the road between the caravans in the caravan park.

The cliff path between here and East Runton Gap has fallen into the sea and the adjacent caravan parks have high steel fences topped with barbed wire. Dense undergrowth and the lack of a path prevent any real attempt at a walk after 40 metres.

Having reached the A149, the walker should exercise care as there is no path on either side until the houses and shops begin. On the northern side the path begins approximately opposite the Methodist Chapel.

At East Runton Gap, marked by a road to the beach and a bingo parlour on the corner, the main road forks to the right. Walk along the footpath beside the main road for 600 metres. The walker passes the bowling green along the left-hand side of the path. At the far side of this is a fence and a public open space. Turn left, i.e. north, along the side of the fence inside the public open space and walk 100 metres to the cliff edge. Turn right and walk along the cliff edge, partly marked by an old road, most of which has fallen into the sea. There is then a walk of 800 metres ($\frac{1}{2}$ mile) along the cliff edge to a raised promenade with a bowling green and putting green on the southern side. At the end of the putting green turn right, cross the main road (Runton Road), and walk along the road opposite, Beach Road. After 300 metres, this reaches Holt Road, the A148. On the right is the entrance to Cromer Beach Railway Station, the official end of the Norfolk Coast Path.

Many may wish to walk back to Sheringham along the Countryside Commission Route, making a walk of 13.9 km ($8\frac{3}{4}$ miles) for the day. Those ending their exploration of the Norfolk Coast Path can catch the train to Norwich either from Sheringham or from Cromer.

Cromer is a difficult town to assess. Looking down from the cliffs to the east or to the west, one sees the wide sands and the pier stretching far into the ocean. At the end of the pier is the lifeboat house. From here Harry Blogg, the famous coxswain of the Cromer Number One boat, set out many score of times in seas few would relish to save the lives of those whose craft could no longer make

The footpath under the railway at East Runton. The route of the Norfolk Coast Path ascends Stone Hill in the background.

passage. Holder of the George Cross and the British Empire Medal, he gained the Royal National Institution's gold medal no fewer than three times. As with many old salts, age did not lessen his ability to master the sea. Like many before him, and many now, he gained that intimate understanding necessary to sail into the swell by fishing for crabs. Those one sees in the pools of Cromer Beach are flotsam the tide has brought in; the bigger ones are caught in pots set out in the shallows.

As in most fishing places, the tower of the church is high: how else would men guide their little craft in? The church is set at the lowest point in the dip between the hills, reflecting the origin of Cromer as an inland settlement; the now lost Shipden was the original fishing village, and only in the fifteenth century did Cromer assume prominence. The juxtaposition of church and main street is unusual for north Norfolk. The bustle of a little town round the church can be disconcerting, and somehow it is a humourless bustle, a reflection of the almost drab late-Victorian surroundings of the town.

Energetic vulgarity motivated the architecture of the 1890s. Cromer has big hotels of this date by a Norwich architect called G.J. Skipper. In his native city he could capture the right spirit: ponderous solemnity for the Norwich Union in 1903, fancy brickwork for his own offices in 1896, or plain exuberance for the Castle entrance to the Royal Arcade. In Cromer, he built the Grand Hotel in 1891, the Hotel Metropole two years later and the Hotel de Paris two years after that; none of them is quite grotesque, but one does wonder what the message is meant to be: looked at from the far end of the pier, the Hotel de Paris resembles the collapsed remains of some enormous multi-tiered wedding cake from which the guests have eaten great lumps before the bride and groom have had the chance to cut it.

Yet behind the town is the setting for one of the more famed of England's country houses, one which is perhaps not as well known as it should be. Felbrigg is a seventeenth-century house, not as grand as those of the eighteenth century such as Holkham Hall or Houghton Hall. Given by a Norfolk writer, Robert Windham Ketton-Cremer, to the National Trust, the house is open to the public. To the south there is a wing built for Thomas Windham in 1620; to the west a wing designed by William Samwell of Watton in the early 1670s for William Windham. The architect died in 1676, but the work was not completed until 1687. The plaster ceiling in the drawing room is of this date, but much of the west wing was remodelled in the 1750s. The fenestration of the west front is distinctly Georgian in style; that of the south front is firmly entrenched in the Elizabethan tradition.

There is more to Felbrigg than just the architecture of the house.

Cromer Pier was built in 1899.

Its contents are a delight, a good but not overpowering collection of paintings, much of which was assembled in the early eighteenth century by a Windham on the Grand Tour, housed in rooms containing contemporary furniture. In the grounds of the house is an orangery which with the adjacent walled garden is the setting for a restored Georgian garden.

It is possible to walk round the grounds of the park, and a Woodland Walk and a Lakeside Walk are both well marked.

Outside the grounds of the house is Felbrigg church. When the Civil War came and men of violence destroyed much of beauty, a thoughtful landowner, Thomas Windham, hurried home from

The memorial to Harry Blogg, coxswain of Cromer lifeboat from 1909 to 1947.

Norwich and gave orders that on no account were Dowsing's men to
be allowed into Felbrigg church. The Windhams had bought the
estate; they had no family connections with the earlier family, the
Felbriggs. To his percipient action we owe the survival of the
impressive series of brasses. These include the memorial of Sir
Simon Felbrigg, standard bearer to Richard II, and his first wife,
erected after her death in 1416. The memorials to the Windhams
follow the successive fashions of the seventeenth, eighteenth and
nineteenth centuries.

Information

DISTANCE	7.7 km/4¾ miles
STATIONS	Sheringham, West Runton, Cromer
BUSES	Sheringham, West Runton, Cromer
ADMISSIONS	Felbrigg: Tuesdays, Wednesdays, Thursdays, Saturdays, Sundays, 14.00–1800 (summer only) Cromer Museum: daily 10.00–12.00, 14.00–17.00
REFRESHMENTS	Sheringham, West Runton, Runton Camp, Cromer
SHOPS	Sheringham, West Runton, East Runton, Cromer
BANKS	Sheringham, West Runton, Cromer
ACCOMMODATION	Sheringham, West Runton, East Runton, Cromer
CAMPING	Beeston Regis, East Runton

Part Four: A Walk from Cromer to Great Yarmouth

The author has devised a walk on similar lines to the Norfolk Coast Path, from Cromer to Great Yarmouth. It follows public footpaths or, on one section, a road, and can easily be used to complete a walk round Norfolk. Sections of it can be enjoyed in their own right. The coast walk was devised as an extension of the Norfolk Coast Path before the establishment of a walk along the former railway line from Aylsham to Stalham via North Walsham. Beginning to the west of Aylsham at Blickling Hall, this walk is known as Weavers Way. It was made an official walk by the Norfolk County Council in 1981 and has become the name for an inland walk from Cromer to Great Yarmouth. This is waymarked by green finger boards.

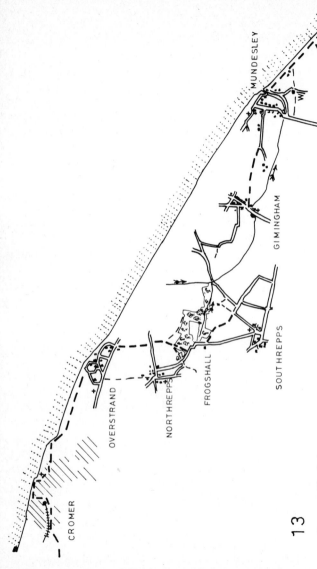

CROMER

OVERSTRAND

NORTHREPPS

FROGSHALL

SOUTHREPPS

GIMINGHAM

MUNDESLEY

13

Cromer to Mundesley

13 Cromer to Mundesley

16.6 km/10¼ miles

The first part of the walk from Cromer to Great Yarmouth is partly along cliff tops and partly inland. From Cromer to Overstrand the route is along the cliff top, but from Overstrand eastwards a number of hazards make cliff-top walking impractical. These include frequent cliff falls, residual World War II sea mines and other coastal defence paraphernalia, particularly at Trimingham and Sidestrand. The inland walk from Overstrand to Mundesley is partly on footpaths and partly on little-used rural roads.

Beginning at Cromer Beach Railway Station, there is more than one practical way to the cliff top on the eastern side of the town. From the ramp at the entry to the station, the walker can first turn left into Holt Road and then left again, into Beach Road and walk north to the sea. After crossing Runton Road, the main A149 road, there is a putting green on the left as one approaches the promenade. Here turn right and walk east, following New Street, to arrive above the pier. At the end of New Street turn right into High Street with Cromer church at the south end on the left. Turn left into Church Street and at the traffic lights turn right into Overstrand Road, the main B1159 road. Pass North Lodge Park, with tennis courts, bowling greens and putting greens, on the left. After this take the third turning on the left into Cliff Lane and walk an ascending 350 metres to the beginning of the cliff-top walk.

Alternatively, the walker can descend the ramp from the railway station and at the junction with Beach Road continue straight ahead along West Street. This leads into Church Street. Thereafter follow the instructions given from Cromer church.

A third alternative is to attempt to walk round the front and the cliffs, thus avoiding the town.

At the top of the path from Cliff Lane there is a memorial to Harry Blogg, Cromer's famous lifeboat coxswain. From this, walk east along the cliff edge for 2.3 km (1½ miles) to Overstrand. The path passes Cromer lighthouse and the golf course beyond. There

Chalk Cliffs between Cromer and Overstrand.

are good views back to the town of Cromer from the lighthouse, which is at a height of 83.5 metres (274 feet). Both before the lighthouse and in the area of the golf course the walker has fairly steep climbs and descents. There are good sea views on this stretch of the walk and interesting geological formations in the cliffs below. Beware of the edge, as this part of East Anglia has been falling into the sea since well before the fifteenth century. In the relatively shallow waters to the north are the remains of a long tongue of land known as Shipden Ness, on which the medieval port of Shipdean was situated. Among the older finds from the Leman and Owers

Banks is a fishing-harpoon head manufactured from deer antler about 8000 BC and now in Norwich Castle Museum.

Further cliff falls will be seen at Overstrand, where the walker comes to the road going inland. Turn right and walk south along this to Overstrand village. There is little point in trying to negotiate the cliff edge further as falls have led to access being prohibited in some areas. In the village, turn left on to the village street and then turn right where the road turns. There is a road ahead, but it has large signs warning of cliff falls ahead and these have recently become more severe. The road shown on the 1:50,000 and 1:25,000 maps no longer exists. After turning right, walk about 200 metres to the main B1159 road and here turn left to walk along the main road for 400 metres.

Overstrand is an interesting relic of the late Victorian and Edwardian era. There are many buildings by the celebrated architect, Sir Edwin Lutyens. At the western end of the village is Overstrand Hall, built in 1899 for a banker, Lord Hillingdon. In the centre of the village is The Pleasaunce, a strange house converted and enlarged from two existing houses. Lutyens did the job for a liberal politician, Cyril Flower, who had been MP for Luton in Bedfordshire and before that a country landowner. In 1893, he became the first Baron Battersea and Overstrand, and proceeded to have a new house built. Both houses are now convalescent homes. Lutyens also designed the Methodist Chapel in Overstrand, on the road from the beach to the village centre, which those walking from Cromer to Great Yarmouth will pass on their right. On the main street of Overstrand, at the eastern end, is another Edwardian house, Sea Marge, very large, with mock half-timbering. Cottages on the main road were also built imitating the style. Overstrand well exemplifies the gross vulgarity and pomposity of the decade of its resurgence.

Quite the most delightful building in the village is the village shop with its iron balcony. Turn right at the top of the road from the beach to see this. The bus stop back into Cromer is opposite.

From Overstrand the walk to Mundesley is inland. The lack of a refreshing sea breeze may be noticeable and the temperature is higher than along the coast.

The Methodist chapel at Overstrand was designed by Sir Edwin Lutyens in 1898. Both the design and the use of brickwork are distinctive.

From the telephone exchange on the B1159 road walk 100 metres east to a public footpath leading south. The houses end here on the main road and there is a bank on the south side of the road. The entrance to the footpath, signposted, is at the beginning of the bank. Turn right into the path, and walk south. After 100 metres go under the bridge of the former Cromer to Mundesley railway, closed in 1953, and continue to walk along the rising path. There is a fork about halfway up the climb; take the left-hand turn to reach the top. If you take the right-hand turn, it will be necessary to walk

east for 100 metres at the top of the hill along a path at the edge of
the scrubland through which this section passes.

On reaching the top of the hill, a tall wireless tower can be seen
prominently to the walker's right 400 metres away. After the
dog-leg exit from the path up the scrubland has been negotiated, the
path becomes better defined with a wide track leading south to the
Northrepps to Sidestrand road. This is a walk of 600 metres. Those
who wish to see the country views are advised to climb the banks on
either side of the path. There is a particularly good view south-west
across to Northrepps village.

At Hungry Hill, on reaching the metalled road, turn left and then
just before the barn turn right on to another footpath leading south.
The walk along the road is only 50 metres. If you wish to visit
Northrepps village, turn right when reaching Hungry Hill. To the
village centre it is a walk of 800 metres ($\frac{1}{2}$ mile).

Northrepps is one of the many flint villages of this part of north
Norfolk. It is not unattractive. The church is large, a reminder of
past prosperity. It was enlarged in the fourteenth century and the
windows were redone in the latter years of the fifteenth century. As
with many Norfolk churches, the most notable feature is the tower,
a landmark which can be seen when looking south from the route
described.

Another landmark is the tower above the north entrance to
Gunton Park. This is shrouded in the trees surrounding the park.
The house at Gunton has been partly demolished following a fire in
1882 and in recent years reconstructed to provide smaller houses in
a sylvan setting. The house was eighteenth-century, with work of
1724 by Matthew Brettingham and of 1785 by James Wyatt, done
for successive members of the Harbord family, the Lords Suffield.
The church just east of the house is by Robert Adam, severely
classical in its inspiration.

The tower is the outstanding building of Gunton. It seems to have
been built in the first half of the nineteenth century as part of an
imposing entry to the park, and is flanked by lodges curving inwards
to the park and outwards to meet the visitor. It is set above a deeply
declining valley, affording an unexpected view from the level drive
to the north side of the tower. Now disused and semi-derelict, the

tower's function appears to be no more than that of a grand
entrance arch, but from the top both the spire of Norwich Cathedral
and the sea can be seen. It is dangerous to ascend.

From the Northrepps to Sidestrand road on Hungry Hill, there is
a walk southwards first beside fields and then through woodland to
Frogshall. After 200 metres the path bears left, and after a further
100 metres the walker should take the right-hand fork. Thereafter
the path begins to descend and become wooded. Good views are to
be had through the woodland. At the second fork, ignore the
right-hand fork and continue straight on, reaching the Northrepps
to Southrepps road after a sharp descent.

At Frogshall there is a road walk of 600 metres after turning left
on to the road. The road first bends right, then left and then right.
After passing Frogshall Farm House there is a crossroads formed by
the road and tracks to the right and the left. Here turn left and walk
beside fields and woodland to the left in an easterly direction.

Frogshall is a pleasant, little-known hamlet: the unpretentious
sort of place it is a joy to discover. On the walk from Frogshall,
there are good views south to Southrepps. Southrepps church is
dominated by a high tower built in the fifteenth century. The church
was extended in the fourteenth century and reduced to its present
aisle-less state in 1791. The village of Southrepps has some good
eighteenth-century houses. To reach Southrepps from the walk,
continue straight on at Frogshall Farm House.

The path going east from Frogshall veers right at the parish
boundary of Northrepps and Southrepps and then left before
meeting the road from Southrepps to Trimingham. Here continue
straight on. After 200 metres, turn left for Trimingham and walk on
a descending road which after 900 metres (just over $\frac{1}{2}$ mile) crosses
Mundesley Beck, a small stream. Ash Tree Farm is before the river
crossing and there is a water-board road to a borehole just after the
crossing. The road then climbs, and 150 metres up the hill there is a
track off to the right just as the road bends slightly to the left. Take
the track and walk along it, skirting a wood after 300 metres. After
a further 400 metres there is a road from Trimingham to
Gimingham; turn right on to this.

Those who miss the track, which is difficult to see, should

A late eighteenth-century farm house at Frogshall.

continue to climb the hill along the narrow road. At the definite fork in the road take the right-hand turn and walk to a crossroads at a former railway bridge. The railway line from Trimingham to Mundesley has mostly been obliterated by the filling in of cuttings and in some cases the levelling of embankments. However, former bridges remain, marked by distinctive brick tops. At the old railway bridge turn sharp right and almost due south on the road from Trimingham to Gimingham.

By following the bends in the road the walker is ultimately heading due east. From the track it is 1.4 km (almost 1 mile) into

The tower at Gunton was part of the north entrance to Gunton Park. It was built in the early nineteenth century.

the village. At the T-junction in the village with council houses opposite, turn right, and then at the road junction by the old school continue straight on. There is a public footpath to the left, three buildings before the watermill at the south end of the village.

Gimingham village school closed in 1980: a common problem in small villages in Norfolk is the loss of the village school. The mill still works, but by motors. By looking over the brick wall of the former wheelhouse, the seating of the mill wheel can be seen. The village pond has swans, ducks and wildfowl. It is possible to walk south along the road from Gimingham to Trunch (see next section).

From Gimingham to Mundesley, the walk is alongside and in some cases across fields. At the signpost marked public footpath, turn left and east. The first part is between the houses, then straight across the first field. At the corner of this field, at its far end, climb two steps up into the higher of the two fields. The difference in their level is about 2 metres. Then walk along the edge of two fields and across a third field. The footpath goes diagonally across a fourth field but it is just as simple to walk round the southern edge of this beside the perimeter fence posts (lacking the fence) of Mundesley Golf Course. From this one has to turn left and then right to the road; if the footpath is followed the road is dead ahead. The road leads into Mundesley village after 1 km (5/8 mile). Ignore the first left-hand turn after the caravan park and continue to a T-junction with the B1145 road. Here turn left and at the T-junction of this and the B1159 road turn right. The Manor House is almost opposite.

Mundesley in the mid-nineteenth century was a small coastal village threatened by erosion. In the 1890s an attempt was made to develop it as a seaside resort, hence the red-brick hotels. The railway came in 1898 and closed in 1959, but the popularity of this quiet resort remained. Subsequently there has been a considerable building boom, mainly of bungalows.

Mundesley church was restored between 1904 and 1914 and a Jacobean pulpit transferred there from Sprowston church. West of the church on the B1159 road back to Trimingham is Beacon Hill, which is 69 metres (226 feet) high. Good views can be obtained from the top.

The cliffs at Mundesley are dramatic, particularly the Paston Cliffs to the east of the village.

At the southern end of Mundesley village, beside the B1159 road, is Stow Mill. This was derelict for some years, but since the early 1970s it has been carefully restored. The brick tower has been repointed, the wooden cap has been restored and repainted and one of the two pairs of sails was mounted on the cap in the summer of 1979. The mill is open to the public and the millstones can be seen.

Information

DISTANCE	16.6 km/10¼ miles
STATION	Cromer
BUSES	Cromer, Overstrand, Mundesley, Northrepps
REFRESHMENTS	Overstrand, Mundesley, Northrepps
SHOPS	Cromer, Overstrand, Northrepps, Mundesley
BANKS	Cromer, Mundesley
ACCOMMODATION	Cromer, Overstrand, Northrepps, Mundesley
CAMPING	Trimingham

14 Mundesley to Sea Palling
18 km/11¼ miles

From Mundesley to Sea Palling it is possible to walk virtually the whole way along the cliff edge, although between Bacton Gas Terminal and Bacton Green it is advisable to head inland. The walk varies from high cliffs to sea level; surfaces include the inner edge of sand dunes, earth on the cliffs and the top of the sea wall.

Standing outside the Manor Hotel in Mundesley face east-south-east. The walk through Mundesley village is along the B1159 road, which dips sharply to cross Mundesley Beck and then rises again with an extremely nasty double bend protected by shoulder-high stone walls. There is no footpath. Walk in single file and be alert for oncoming traffic.

At the top of the hill on the east side of Mundesley Beck there is a sharp right-hand turn and a straight road approaches this. Drivers who are unfamiliar with the area often arrive at the corner much too fast. This road going south has a footpath and can be used by those who wish to visit the windmill at Stow Hill (see previous section).

Those walking along the cliffs should cross the main road at the corner mentioned and begin walking south-east along the cliff edge path. There are a few bungalows on the landward side of the path. After 700 metres a timber-built holiday camp can be observed. About 100 metres beyond this there is a metalled road heading west back to Mundesley windmill. After this the path becomes narrower but is still well defined and walkable for the 800 metres (½ mile) to the western fence of the Bacton Natural Gas Terminal.

Bacton Natural Gas Terminal was built in 1957 to act as the inshore collection place for gas piped from the North Sea. It is a fine example of modern engineering. On the south side of the B1159 road is a further complex, the British Gas Distribution Station. From here runs the underground pipeline which the walker crossed on Peddars Way near Stonebridge.

At the gas terminal the walker has two choices. The first alternative is to walk along the cliff on the seaward side of the

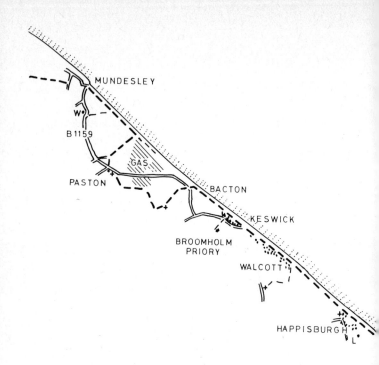

MUNDESLEY

W

B 1159

GAS

PASTON

BACTON

KESWICK

BROOMHOLM
PRIORY

WALCOTT

HAPPISBURGH
L

14

Mundesley to Sea Palling (the above maps should be read as adjacent to each other,
ie. the route after Happisburgh follows on to Walcott)

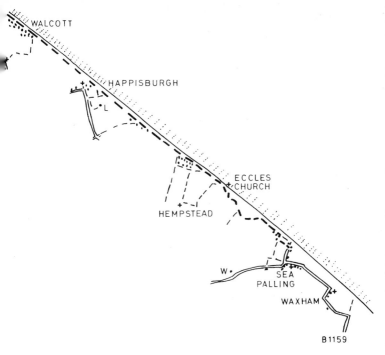

WALCOTT

HAPPISBURGH

L

ECCLES
CHURCH

HEMPSTEAD

W

SEA
PALLING

WAXHAM

B 1159

terminal. This is quite safe as there is a 50-metre-wide area between the fence surrounding the industrial buildings and the cliff edge. A firm path has been beaten along this about 10 to 20 metres from the cliff edge. It heads for the seaward end of the fence on the eastern side of the Bacton Natural Gas Terminal. This fence overhangs the cliff edge by about 1 metre (3 feet) and to continue it is necessary to abseil round the fence, with only the fence itself for support. Those brave enough to do this will then find a path along the cliff edge for a further 200 metres. At the end of this turn right and head south alongside a fence to the main road. At the road turn left and walk 30 metres to where the road veers right. Follow the road for 200 metres and then take a left-hand fork which leads to the beginning of the sea wall from Bacton to Walcott. If the walker misses this turning, he can walk into Bacton Green where the houses begin and the road turns right, a further 350 metres along the road. Here turn left along a road signposted to the sea, and at the sea defences turn right.

The second alternative from the west side of the Bacton Natural Gas Terminal is to turn right on to a footpath heading south-west to Paston village. Walk along this for 800 metres ($\frac{1}{2}$ mile) and at the end bear left on to a metalled road leading to Paston Hall. At the crossroads by Paston Hall turn left on to the main road and walk past the barn, the church and Hall Farm, which is north of the main road, to a right-hand turn signposted for Bacton church. Here turn right and follow this road to Bacton church. From Paston, the road first bears left and then turns left before becoming straight for 400 metres, after which it veers right and then at Lowlands Farm turns right. At Church Farm the walker will meet a T-junction. Here turn left and, where the metalled road turns right, continue dead ahead for 50 metres to the church. From Bacton church there is a good footpath heading north-east to Bacton Green. On meeting the B1159, turn right and then walk on the road to the sea. At the sea defences turn right to face south-east to walk to Walcott and beyond.

The advantage of walking inland at the Bacton Natural Gas Terminal is that it enables the walker to visit a number of interesting places. Paston was the home before the fifteenth century of the Paston family. In the fifteenth century some members moved away from Norfolk, and their letters to and from home form the basis of the well-known *Paston Letters*, one of the fullest sources for the social history of the age. The Pastons were country gentry whose fortunes rose on the profits first of the wool trade and later of farming. At Paston they built a great house, now demolished. The present Paston Hall, now an hotel, is an eighteenth-century building with stucco walls. North of the hall is a barn built of flint with brick quoins, buttresses and jambs. It was erected by Sir William Paston in 1581. It is 49.7 metres (163 feet) long, 7.32 metres (24 feet) wide and 18.3 metres (60 feet) high. The roof is externally of reed thatch; internally the roof timbers are alternatively tie-beams and hammer-beams. On request, the barn can be viewed. St Margaret's church, Paston, has a thatched roof and was built in the fourteenth century. The roof timbers are a single span of 9.67 metres (29 feet 6 inches); their unusual construction is known as a scissor-beam roof, whereby the thrust is transferred across to the opposite wall. Various members of the Paston family are commemorated by memorials in the chancel, including two sculptures by Nicholas Soane: a Jacobean figure tomb of 1629 for Dame Katherine Paston and a plain urn done in 1632 to commemorate Sir Edmund Paston, her husband.

On the west side of Paston Great Barn a road going south and then south-east leads to Knapton. Knapton is another splendid Norfolk village, a little off the tourist trail. The chief glory, of course, is the double hammer-beam roof to the church of St Peter and St Paul, installed in 1503 by John Smithe. There is a font cover with a Greek inscription of 1704, set oddly on a thirteenth-century font of Purbeck marble, but notice high in the roof above the font the setting for a pulley wheel to raise an older font cover, contemporary no doubt with the roof. It would have been this earlier cover which Richard Howes, one of the author's ancestors, raised to baptise his own children and those of his parishioners. Richard Howes, Rector of Knapton, was ejected from the living in 1643 for his views incompatible with Puritan doctrine.

Walking west from Knapton, one comes to Trunch. Do not be put off by the hideous 1930s brick box of a public house, for Trunch is one of the most attractive flint-built villages in Norfolk. Externally the church is unprepossessing; internally it is a joy to behold, with a superb collection of early sixteenth-century woodwork: separating the chancel from the nave is a screen of 1502 and high above the nave is a hammer-beam roof of delicate construction. These are minor works compared with that facing the south door, a font canopy. There are three others in England including that in the church of St Peter Mancroft high above Norwich market-place. Trunch font canopy is hexagonal with a hexagonal canopied top and is covered in carvings.

Those with a day to spare could walk round these villages – Paston, Knapton and Trunch – to savour the beauty of a quiet,

The chapter house of Broomholm Priory retains part of the thirteenth-century arcade above the monks' stalls.

unravished part of England. Further south is North Walsham, the local town, now somewhat expanded. Nelson went to school here at Paston Grammar School, founded in 1606 by the builder of Paston Great Barn, Sir William Paston, who died two years later and is buried beneath an alabaster monument in St Nicholas's church on the other side of the market place from his school. The church is large and has a number of interesting survivals: a communion table of Edward VI's reign, a dual set of royal arms (one side commemorating Oliver Cromwell, the other Charles II), and a fifteenth-century font cover with its own hanging beam but otherwise modern roofs. The tower is in ruins after falls in 1724 and 1835. On the market place is the Market Cross, built after a fire in 1600 and restored in 1897.

The modern parish of Bacton, which includes Broomholm and Keswick, has a number of monuments. The church of St Andrew, passed on the inland walk from Paston, has a thatched chancel; inside there is an octagonal font with the symbols of the evangelists carved on four of the faces and shields held by angels on the other four. The village, strung out along the B1159, has a number of old houses. The most distinctive, near to 'The King's Arms' public house, is the so-called Pilgrims' House, built of flint with brick facings and having an overhanging first floor. It is opposite the entry to Bacton Abbey Farm. Broomholm Priory, founded in 1113, is also known as Bacton Abbey. It can be visited on request to the farmhouse, preferably by prior appointment. The gatehouse is at the end of a drive lined with cottages. Buses turn round in the large space beside the main road. Remaining of the abbey buildings are a two-storey north transept of twelfth-century date and a thirteenth-century chapter house with very fine blind arcading. Much of these are now used as a farm store. Keswick village is one of a number of places along the coast which have been swallowed by the sea.

From Bacton Green, the northern end of the village of Bacton beside the sea, it is possible to walk along the sea defences for 2.8 km (1¾ miles). This walk takes one along the seaward side of Bacton and Keswick, parallel with the main B1159 road at Walcott Gap and beside the caravan parks at Walcott. Walcott church is inland, 1.2 km (¾ mile) south along the B1159 road. Struck by lightning in 1961 and subsequently restored, All Saints' church, Walcott, is notable for its tall windows and upstanding tower, originally constructed towards the end of the fourteenth century.

At the end of the sea defences, the route becomes a footpath ascending the cliffs. Follow this for 1.6 km (1 mile) to Happisburgh. The village name is pronounced Haze-brer; the spelling derives from the ancient Happing Hundred, an administrative division used from before the Norman Conquest until the Victorian period.

Before the lighthouse was built in 1791, the fifteenth-century tower of Happisburgh church served to warn sailors of the dangerous waters beneath the cliffs. The tower is 33.55 metres (110 feet) high. The churchyard is almost on the edge of the sea. The large size of the church, which was rebuilt twice before the fifteenth century, indicates the prosperity of the village in the Middle Ages, part of which was due to Happisburgh's position as the meeting place of Happing Hundred, one of the thirty-three hundreds (ancient territorial divisions) of the county of Norfolk.

Happisburgh cliffs include much sand in their make-up and need protection from erosion by the sea.

Happisburgh church stands high above the cliffs but sufficiently inland to be safe from erosion. The tower is 33.55 metres (110 feet) high and acted as a lighthouse before the present lighthouse was built in 1791. Happisburgh Sands to the north and east of the parish are a notorious graveyard for shipping. The lighthouse is further inland and set on another knoll. Its distinctive red and white bands can be seen from long distances away: I have seen it from Beeston Bump, to the west, and from Winterton church, to the south. The lighthouse is 41.5 metres (136 feet) high with a sequence of three flashes every 30 seconds. It is on an isolated site; the main village is around the church and on the road to the coastguard station. Happisburgh Manor, designed by Detmar Blow in 1900, has four diagonally-placed wings to a central core.

Approaching Happisburgh from the north-west by the path along the cliff edge the walker would miss the village, as after crossing a small caravan site he comes out above the path leading from the coastguard and lifeboat stations to the sea. Here he should turn right and walk south to a metalled road where he turns left and goes east to rejoin the coastal walk. The lighthouse is first dead ahead and then to one's right.

All the way from Walcott there are good views back along the coast. Mundesley is clearly visible. Below are groynes and other sea defences constructed after the 1953 floods. They were completed in 1956.

From Happisburgh to Sea Palling the walker has a more difficult walk than hitherto. From the metalled road continue south-east along the cliff edge for 500 metres. In places the road has fallen into the sea and it is necessary to walk on the inner edge of the field. The route is established, and along a public right of way but take care not to destroy crops. At a wireless station with towers turn right and inland to a track leading inside the sand dunes. After 150 metres turn left and follow the track south-east. At times there are wooden bungalows between the track and the sand dunes to the north-east. After 1.2 km (1¼ miles), where a large estate of holiday chalets begins, turn right to walk south and when these end turn left and east along their southern edge. Walk along this track for 800 metres (½ mile) to the sand dunes and then veer right to walk along the track on the inner edge of the sand dunes for 500 metres. This is Manor Farm, Eccles, approached by a metalled road from the south. At the metalled road turn left; at the gap in the dunes turn right along the path which continues on the inner edge of the dunes.

The gap in the dunes is North Gap, the better of the two entries to the beach to examine the two surviving rocks of Eccles Church. The sea destroyed the body of the church in the Middle Ages, but the tower stood until 1895 when, on 23 January, it crashed to the ground during a terrible storm. Between 1953 and 1983 the

The village of Eccles was already 'ruinated by the sea' in 1605. The tower of the church stood until it was blown down in a gale in January 1895. All that remained in July 1979, when this photograph was taken, were two blocks of stone almost buried in the sand and barely distinguishable from their surroundings.

surviving portions have become more and more buried in the sands.

From North Gap to Sea Palling, the path is partly away from the dunes. From North Gap head south and then turn left with the path which goes east for 200 metres. There turn right and follow the path first south and then south-east past Castle Farm, approached by another metalled road. Ignoring all turnings to the left, continue on the path to the dunes, where turn right, passing a succession of

wooden chalets and bungalows. After 800 metres ($\frac{1}{2}$ mile), there is a
right-hand turn. Take this in preference to walking straight on,
where there is a poor surface for walking. Having turned right, turn
left after 200 metres and walk south-east for 300 metres to reach
Cart Gap, a metalled road, leading from Sea Palling to the beach.
Here turn right and walk 400 metres to the main B1159 road.
Opposite will be seen the village sign of Sea Palling in front of the
local garage.

Sea Palling is a summer-only holiday resort; the locals call it
'Pauling'. Interesting geological formations are visible on the beach
at Sea Palling. The church, set behind the village, has a wide nave
incorporating a former nave and aisles of the same width; the
alteration was made in the fifteenth century.

Information

DISTANCE	18 km/$11\frac{1}{4}$ miles
STATIONS	none
BUSES	Mundesley, Bacton, Walcott, Happisburgh, Sea Palling
REFRESHMENTS	Mundesley, Bacton, Walcott, Happisburgh, Sea Palling
SHOPS	Mundesley, Bacton, Walcott, Happisburgh, Sea Palling
BANKS	Mundesley
ACCOMMODATION	Mundesley, Bacton, Walcott, Happisburgh, Sea Palling
CAMPING	Sea Palling

15 Sea Palling to Winterton-on-Sea
12 km/7½ miles

From Sea Palling to Winterton there is no satisfactory alternative to a walk along the B1159 road from Sea Palling at least as far as Horsey Corner. In some ways the best route is to follow the road from Sea Palling to Somerton and then to walk along a bridleway to Winterton-on-Sea. There is a footpath from Warren Farm, at TG/460246, to Winterton-on-Sea, but this is a difficult walk through sand dunes for part of the way.

From the village sign at Sea Palling, outside the garage, face east and walk for 1.2 km (¾ mile) to Waxham, which consists of a hall, a small church, a large barn and a farm. The hall is of various dates including an Elizabethan block and a fifteenth-century gatehouse on the northern side. The church has a ruined chancel with a small area now railed off for the altar. There is a monument of 1571 to Thomas Wodehouse on the northern side. The farm is unexceptional but the barn is larger in floor area than that at Paston. It is 60 cm (2 ft) shorter but 3.65 metres (12 ft) wider, with a great high roof, covered with reed thatch. The full dimensions of Waxham barn are impressive: length 49 metres (161 feet), width 11 metres (36 feet). It is built of flint with quoins, jambs and buttresses of stone and brick. The end wall has a diaper of brick set in the flint. Its date is probably sixteenth-century, although the roof structure suggests at least a century earlier.

After Waxham barn, turn left following the main road which bends a little in the next 800 metres (½ mile) before a right-hand turn. It is possible to reach the beach by turning left here, as it is from walking along the track beside Waxham churchyard. The sand dunes here are called the Marram Hills. Good views of these may be obtained from walking south to Brograve Farm, where one bears left and then left again and after 150 metres turns right, so as to face south-east. From Brograve Farm the walker has a 2.2 km (1½ miles) walk to Horsey Corner, a right-angled right-hand turn on the main road. The scenery is interesting, with farmland between the road

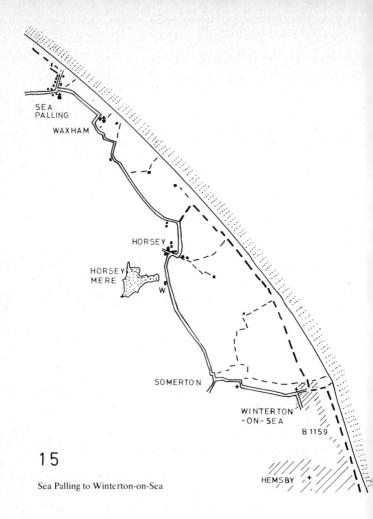

SEA
PALLING

WAXHAM

HORSEY

HORSEY
MERE

W

SOMERTON

WINTERTON
-ON-SEA

B 1159

HEMSBY

15

Sea Palling to Winterton-on-Sea

and the sea on the north-eastern side and the edge of the Broads on the south-western side.

At Horsey Corner there are two alternatives. For a walk through the sand dunes, turn left and walk 800 metres to the sea. Here turn right and head south-east along a path through the sand dunes to Winterton-on-Sea. Part of this is a difficult walk. It also involves climbing a slight hill, Bramble Hill, which because of the terrain presents more difficulties than would appear at first sight. Although it is marked on the map, the author would not always recommend this route.

For the walk along the main road, at Horsey Corner turn right and walk south for 800 metres ($\frac{1}{2}$ mile). The right-hand turn of the road brings the walker into Horsey village. The public house, 'Nelson's Head', is at the far end of the left-hand turn of the village. The church is at the far end to the west: nave and chancel are in one, under a thatched roof.

The road makes two small left-hand turns at the end of Horsey village before heading south-east to West Somerton. After 800 metres ($\frac{1}{2}$ mile), the walker will be abreast of Horsey Mill, a drainage mill, built in 1912. Horsey Mere, an offshoot of the Broads, is 150 metres down the footpath which leads east from the gate at the northern end of the car park beside Horsey Mill. Cap and sails remain on the mill.

Horsey Mere and 600 hectares (1,500 acres) of surrounding land are National Trust property. Looking east across the water Stubb Mill can be seen, another drainage mill but lacking its sails, as is the drainage mill visible north-east of Horsey Mere on the edge of Brayden Marshes. Good bird-watching is to be had at Horsey Mere.

From the windmill beside the B1159 road, it is a walk of 2.7 km ($1\frac{1}{2}$ miles) to the hamlet of West Somerton. This is interesting as a small hamlet on the edge of the Broads. The village sign is wrought iron, not the usual wooden carving. At West Somerton ascend the quite steep hill past the school and at the top turn left and walk along the main road for 700 metres (about $\frac{1}{2}$ mile). The road then turns right and then left, but it is possible to walk straight on past the site of St Mary's church, East Somerton. The bridlepath leads across fields to Winterton-on-Sea. At the end of the bridlepath, by

Winter ploughing at Winterton-on-Sea. The church tower was raised in the fifteenth century to its present height of 39 metres (130 feet). From here the lighthouse and church tower at Happisburgh can be seen.

the edge of the dunes, turn right into Winterton village. After 250 metres turn right. Winterton-on-Sea bus turning circle is reached after 50 metres.

The two Somerton villages and Winterton-on-Sea are linked by their names. Somerton was the place of the summer pastures; at Winterton, sheep and cattle were kept during the winter. Winterton can be a bleak place on a cold day. The church has a very tall tower, heightened in the fifteenth century to provide a beacon to shipping.

From beside the church the view north is stunning. In the distance can be seen Walcott and Happisburgh church towers and Happisburgh lighthouse.

If the walker turns right at Somerton school, he will come to Martham after a walk of 2 km (1¼ miles). Martham has a farm museum at Church Farm and a pleasant village green with interesting houses set round it. The church of St Mary was rebuilt between 1855 and 1861. Philip Boyce of Cheltenham was the architect chosen by Mrs Dawson, who paid for the rebuilding, including the new hammer-beam roof, copying the old one. Again, looking north from the village there are good views both over the Broads and of distant church and lighthouse towers.

Information

DISTANCE	12 km/7½ miles
STATIONS	none
BUSES	Sea Palling, Somerton, Winterton-on-Sea
REFRESHMENTS	Sea Palling, Horsey, West Somerton, Winterton-on-Sea
SHOPS	Horsey, West Somerton, Winterton-on-Sea
BANKS	Martham
ACCOMMODATION	Sea Palling, Winterton-on-Sea, Martham
CAMPING	Winterton-on-Sea, Sea Palling, Waxham, Horsey

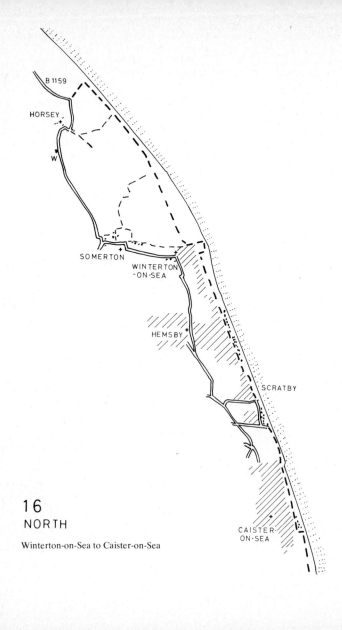

B 1159

HORSEY

W

SOMERTON

WINTERTON
-ON-SEA

HEMSBY

SCRATBY

CAISTER-
ON-SEA

16
NORTH

Winterton-on-Sea to Caister-on-Sea

16 Winterton-on-Sea to Great Yarmouth
16.4 km/10¼ miles

The final section of the walk along the Norfolk coast from Cromer
to Great Yarmouth begins in the sand dunes of Winterton-on-Sea
and ends at the north pier of Yarmouth harbour. Between these the
walker will climb to the top of the sand cliffs of Scratby, Newport,
California and Caister-on-Sea before descending to the very long
front of Great Yarmouth. Despite many modern developments
along the coast, including holiday chalets at Hemsby Gap (also
known as Newport) and holiday camps at Caister, for most of the
way it is possible to walk along the edge of the land and diversions
inland are rare.

At Winterton-on-Sea bus turning circle, face east and walk along
the road to the beach, a distance of 70 metres, passing first
Victorian houses and then on the extreme edge of the sand dunes
some more recent houses. The track becomes progressively more
sandy as the easterly winds bring sand off the beach and from the
dunes on to the concreted track. At the end of the track there is a
car park beside the coastguard look-out station. There is usually
also a small tea-stall caravan parked on the hard standing. Beside
the car park and set in the dunes are large concrete blocks built into
the landscape for coastal protection. Winterton beach is dangerous
for bathing, as notices proclaim and warning flags indicate.

At the concrete blocks turn right to face south and begin the walk
through the dunes. For the first 800 metres (½ mile) this is not an
easy path to follow along the ridge of the dunes on the landward
side of the beach. There are several well-beaten tracks, as the walk
from Hemsby to Winterton is a popular one with holiday makers.
Any one of these can be followed. After about 1 km (5/8 mile) the
first holiday chalet will be encountered. For the next 3.2 km (2
miles) these are a constant feature of the landscape. In the vicinity
of the first holiday chalets, the path along the top of the sand dunes
becomes less easy to negotiate, mainly owing to the property rights
of the chalets. However, this is where the path on the inner edge of

the dunes becomes more clearly visible, and there are several paths
down from the top of the dunes to the path inside the dunes.

Follow the path inside the dunes thereafter for 2.4 km ($1\frac{1}{2}$ miles).
The sea is not visible for much of this path but until Hemsby Gap,
where there are many chalets on the seaward side, it is a pleasant
walk through a wide valley with interesting fauna and flora. After a
while it becomes progressively narrower until at Hemsby Gap the
path is only 20 metres wide, whereas further north it is up to 60
metres wide.

Hemsby Gap has bingo and much else of the candy-floss culture
of the late twentieth century, but it has been an established holiday
centre for well over fifty years. Hemsby village is 1.2 km ($\frac{3}{4}$ mile)
inland. The fourteenth-century church, dedicated to St Mary, has
nave and chancel under a single roof. The fenestration of the nave
was renewed in the fifteenth century but only the east window of the
chancel was enlarged. The original timbering of the roof, chiefly the
bosses in the nave, is of similar date. Despite the fairly modern rood
screen, the interior gives an impression of great length as there is no
chancel arch. In Hemsby village there is an early Victorian farm-
labourer's cottage restored as part of European Architectural
Heritage Year, 1975. It is timber-framed with timber clapboarding
as the walls.

From Hemsby Gap, follow the path south along the valley behind
the dunes. Part of this is metalled for vehicular access to the holiday
chalets. These continue for 800 metres ($\frac{1}{2}$ mile). At the end of the
chalets, there is an ascending path which reaches the top of Newport
Cliffs at a house known as 'Cottage on the Cliff'. Walk
south-south-east along the sand cliffs for 800 metres ($\frac{1}{2}$ mile). There
are houses, mostly of the 1930s and 1950s, on the inner edge of the
road beside the cliffs. The road is separated from the cliff edge by a
wide green sward. There are good sea views from here.

At the end of the sward the road goes inland between houses to
California. At the end of the road turn left and after 30 metres turn
right to walk along the road beside the cliff edge. This metalled,
main road veers due south after 20 metres and thereafter has
buildings on both sides. On the western side, to the walker's right, is
a holiday camp. Walk south for 600 metres to a T-junction with a

road running west to east. Here turn left and walk east to the cliff edge. At the cliff edge turn right and walk south-south-east along the cliff edge path, exercising care. The path is fairly wide and it is possible to walk along the route of the former Midland and Great Northern Joint Railway line which between California and Caister-on-Sea ran very close to the cliff edge.

California is the seaside edge of Scratby. Scratby has long been united as an ecclesiastical and civil parish with Great Ormesby, more usually known as Ormesby St Margaret. All Saints' church at Scratby disappeared before the sixteenth century and the parishioners went inland to St Margaret's church at Ormesby, on the south-eastern side of the village. Most of the church is Victorian refurbishing, but there is an original twelfth-century south door. Ormesby had another church, dedicated to St Peter, on its western side, but this has long been demolished. The village was the home of the Yarmouth brewing and banking family, the Lacons, who lived in Ormesby Hall, the fine Georgian house immediately to the east of the church. There are other eighteenth-century houses in Ormesby: Ormesby House, set in trees near the village centre, and The Grange at East End, at the northern end of the Caister by-pass. Inland from Ormesby St Margaret is Ormesby St Michael, or Little Ormesby. The church has a thatched nave. The A149 connecting these villages continues west and after 2 km (1¼ miles) crosses a causeway between Ormesby Broad to the north and Rollesby Broad to the south. Go there on a late autumn afternoon and watch the sun set. It is the best time to walk round the Fleggs, the area to the north of Yarmouth, thick with names ending in '-by', indicative of the Scandinavian settlement of the years after 879. The numerous 'thorpe' names are also Danish in origin.

The name of Caister-on-Sea is much older: there was a walled Romano-British town here in the first to fourth centuries AD. Remains can be seen on the north side of the Norwich road, 50 metres west of Holy Trinity church. About 1.2 km (¾ mile) west of the Roman town is Caister Castle, built in the 1430s by Sir John Fastolf 'out of the profits of the French wars': the knight was the leading English general of his day and amassed a great fortune from plunder and ransoms. This he used to construct a large mansion in

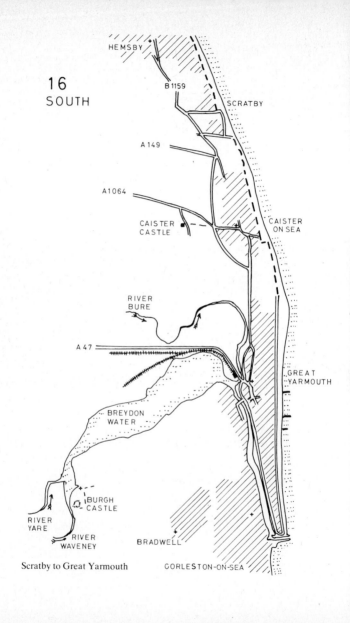

HEMSBY

B1159

SCRATBY

A149

A1064

CAISTER
CASTLE

CAISTER
ON SEA

RIVER
BURE

A47

GREAT
YARMOUTH

BREYDON
WATER

BURGH
CASTLE

RIVER
YARE

RIVER
WAVENEY

BRADWELL

GORLESTON-ON-SEA

Scratby to Great Yarmouth

Caister Castle is one of the showpieces of late medieval domestic architecture. It was built by Sir John Fastolf, one of King Henry V's captains in France, in the then newly fashionable material, brick. Beyond the great hall is a tower from which Sir John could see the lands of all his estates, both north and south of Breydon Water.

the latest style using the latest building material, brick. Of this only the west tower and adjacent curtain walls survive, but it is still no mean structure. The tower is all of 30 metres (98 feet) high, its stair turret higher still and the great walls are still half-way up the sides of the tower. All are crowned by machicolations, a projecting series of brick-built brackets designed to hold a gallery, though at Caister Castle – as with other early brick buildings – the intention was much more to demonstrate the brickmaker's art.

Caister-on-Sea is now a dormitory village for Great Yarmouth, but there is a thriving holiday industry based on more than one holiday camp. The church of Holy Trinity is thirteenth-century. Inside there is a seventeenth-century commandment board with Moses and Aaron flanking the words. In the cemetery on the other side of the village street from the church is a memorial to the lifeboatmen who died attempting a rescue on 14 November 1901.

The short section of 1.7 km (about 1 mile) from Caister Point to the northern end of the promenade at Great Yarmouth is difficult to follow. There is no firm path and the former railway line is now partly overgrown. Walkers are advised to pick their way through the sand dunes with the beach to their left, i.e. on the eastern side. From the northern end of the promenade at Great Yarmouth, the route follows the road along the seashore. After about 1.6 km (1 mile), it is possible to walk along the outer promenade with gardens, bowling greens and seaside attractions to the walker's right. There is then a walk of 5.2 km (3¼ miles) along the promenade to the North Pier and the entry to the River Yare to the sea.

Forget the gaudy razzle-dazzle of the short sea-front where the action is. Behind the cheap knick-knacks and the candy-floss, Yarmouth presents a very different face, of an elegant town with ladies in fur coats who can afford the best dressmakers and the finest china. With over 50,000 people living within the old borough, it is the centre for the farming community of the Fleggs to the north and Lothingland to the south. The herring port of yesteryear – its heyday was the decade before the Great War – has turned to timber and general freight, and the container lorries roll on and roll off the twice-daily run to Rotterdam, while where the smacks and drifters were welded and fashioned, most unsealike structures rise, those modern leviathans, the rigs and platforms of the offshore oil business.

Yarmouth, too, is an old town: Defoe called it 'an ancient place'. Nelson and Dickens came here for holidays. The admiral left from the jetty before the battle of Copenhagen, and the town later honoured the memory of the boy from Norfolk with a column on the South Denes in 1817. *David Copperfield* was written at the Royal Hotel in 1843; the novel abounds in local colour. There are

Charles Dickens wrote much of *David Copperfield* at the Royal Hotel, Great Yarmouth, in 1843. The hotel was the first building on the sea front specifically designed to attract visitors to the town. Previously the area between the town walls and the sea had been used as net-drying grounds.

hotels of their times on the front. Then Great Yarmouth appealed to a select clientele as it still did when the main body of the buildings on the front were erected. The Edwardian seaside town is not difficult to find among more modern additions. Of various styles, the façades of the theatres were distinctly showy; now they have become acceptable with age but this is an acceptance they did not universally command among architectural critics when they were built. The exuberance of some which were condemned as

The mouth of the River Yare is south of the long spit of the town of Great Yarmouth. On the west bank is the separate town of Gorleston, whose church tower can be seen in the centre.

outrageous and lacking in taste now seems a neat contrast to the solemn and ponderous Victorian façades, set as they are in close proximity.

Until the Victorian age, the area east of the old town walls was sand dunes used as the drying ground for herring nets. The old town is a very small place, enclosed by a wall, still virtually complete, which takes rather more than an hour to walk round. No gates survive, but most of the towers do. Some have Tudor additions to

their fourteenth-century structures: Yarmouth was refortified by
Henry VIII in 1545 and by Elizabeth I in 1588. Inside the walls,
three streets run from north to south. Between them ran the
Yarmouth Rows; more are marked by blue plaques than actually
survive. They were a system of town planning of the sixteenth
century or earlier, designed to enclose everyone within the walls.
The town was then based on the river. Here were the finest houses,
many of which are now offices, though No. 4 South Quay is open to
the public as the Elizabethan House Museum. Others are of the
eighteenth century, including the Customs House, built for John
Andrews out of the profits of the herring trade.

At the northern end of the quay is the town hall. J.B. Pearce
produced the winning design in a competition in 1881. One grows
to like it, perhaps because it does not fall into the trap of being a
pastiche. The bridge to the north connects Yarmouth with
Southtown and the main road to London. The present bridge, the
third on the site, was opened in 1931. Stand on it and look down the
river: Defoe's description of it as the finest quay in England still
holds good. He considered it to be better than that at Marseilles. In
prospect, it is markedly superior to the India Quay in Seville. North
of the bridge the river turns west and the tide ebbs south into
Breydon Water, the sight of which refreshes the mind of a
care-worn man.

Inside the town a strict segregation of houses and market was
formerly enforced: now the shops extend much further south than
the market place. If not as grand in the formal sense as that in
Northampton, the market-place at Yarmouth would not be out of
place in the Netherlands or north Germany. Of an informal shape,
neatly closed at the south by roads which follow the line of the river
bank, it has other echoes of the Dutch connection. St Nicholas's, the
principal and indeed until 1716 the only church of Yarmouth, lies
screened to the north, with Church Plain to its south and White
Horse Plain to its west, extensions of the market place. A great barn
of a building, the narrow nave of the Norman plan made to seem
more miniscule by the excessively wide naves (at 13 metres – 39 feet
– the widest in England), St Nicholas's church was
unsympathetically restored following damage by fire bombs in

1942. The interior woodwork includes much from the eighteenth-century St George's church, now closed for worship and used as a civic arts centre. Set amid the snarl of Yarmouth traffic and now skilfully restored, St George's church, designed by John Price in 1714 and opened two years later, is one of the most memorable buildings of Yarmouth, not only because it stands so proudly on the ridge which is the sandspit on which the town is built. Looking west from the church, the visitor can see Yarmouth House, with its top like three great malt-kilns, a reminder that Yarmouth was an important brewing town. Beside this is the new public library of 1961, a sensible, light, airy place grafted on to the end of the Tolhouse, a thirteenth-century house now restored as a museum. The Tolhouse, originally a private house, has had many functions: council room, court house, jail, with the dungeons surviving as a very realistic exhibit.

To walk round Yarmouth could take a day. Those who have walked to the north pier can retrace their steps along the South Quay past the oil tanks, the power station, the cranes and the herring merchants' houses and then from Hall Quay walk north along North Quay to the bridge which leads across the River Bure to Vauxhall railway station. The walker who has followed the route across Norfolk from Thetford along Peddars Way to Holme-next-the-Sea, and then walked round the Norfolk coast from Hunstanton to Cromer and then on to Great Yarmouth, may take away as a final impression of the county the view across Breydon Water.

Information

DISTANCE	16.4 km/10¼ miles
STATION	Great Yarmouth
BUSES	Winterton-on-Sea, Hemsby, Caister-on-Sea, Great Yarmouth
ADMISSIONS	Caister Castle: June–September, daily except Saturdays 10.30–17.30
REFRESHMENTS	Winterton-on-Sea, Hemsby, Caister-on-Sea, Great Yarmouth

SHOPS	Winterton-on-Sea, Hemsby, Caister-on-Sea, Great Yarmouth
BANKS	Martham, Hemsby (restricted days), Caister-on-Sea, Great Yarmouth
ACCOMMODATION	Winterton-on-Sea, Hemsby, Caister-on-Sea, Great Yarmouth
CAMPING	Winterton-on-Sea, Hemsby, Caister-on-Sea, Great Yarmouth

Index